FUNNY BONES

Health & Humor Specialists

Funnybones

Funnybones
Health & Humor Specialists

Royal Publishing, Inc.
P.O. Box 1120
18825 Hicrest Road
Glendora, California 91740

Library of Congress Cataloging in Publication Date in Progress.

ISBN 0-934344-27-2

Printed in the United States of America

"A cheerful heart is good medicine."

- Proverbs 17:22

FUNNY BONES

CONTENTS

Steve Allen, Jr., M.D.
Stress Management - Creative Juggling
735 Watkins Road
Horseheads, NY 14845
(yes, there is such a place)

Steve Allen, Jr., M.D.

Steve Allen, Jr., M.D. delights thousands of people each year with his lighthearted look at stress. His programs blend his expertise as a Board Certified Family Physician and his natural heritage of wit into a valuable and entertaining presentation. Steve emphasizes the special value of laughter and play in not only reducing the body's unpleasant reactions to stress but in preventing these reactions as well.

A 1970 honor graduate of the University of Southern California School of Medicine, Steve has received training in family medicine, internal medicine, adolescent medicine, counseling, and human sexuality. He continues his eleventh year in medical practice in upstate New York, and travels extensively lecturing on stress and human sexuality. His programs and his innovative practice earned the 1983 Award for Outstanding Contributions to Preventive Health from the New York State Federation of Professional Health Educators.

Steve's unique approach to stress management has its roots in his family's gift of humor. His grandmother Belle Montrose was in the circus before her career in vaudeville with Steve's grandfather Billy Allen. The echo of comedian (and father) Steve Allen's laugh can be recognized as Dr. Steve Allen, Jr. teaches everyone in the audience to juggle brightly colored scarves as they learn to play and laugh their way to a more stress free life.

Foreword

By Steve Allen, Jr., M.D.

Humor — is it good for what ails you or just a momentary pleasant event? That's an odd question, if not actually a downright funny one.

I think humor, laughter and playfulness are on the list of age old methods that reduce stress and add a little perspective to our day. They join sitting in hot water, massage, exercise, and appropriate diet, relaxation, prayer, and meditation as time-honored methods of recreation. I use "recreation" in its old-fashioned sense of re-creating your energy for the trials and work of life.

Laughter, play and humor have been around since humans started recording their thoughts on papyrus. Actually, humor started before recorded history. The lovely paintings of animals on the walls of caves in France are considered to be human's earliest examples of aesthetically beautiful art. However, Kevin Wofsy, a 15-year-old humorist in San Francisco, thinks they were cartoons drawn by kids who were bored at the time. His guess is that they were probably bugging their mother who, while cleaning a brontosaurus, undoubtedly said, "Find something to do! Why don't you use those new things your grandmother invented called 'paints.' Go draw something!" As you know, of course there were no easels or paper or canvas or even a refrigerator to hang them on when they were through, so they used the cave walls.

They hadn't invented the cartoon balloon to show what the animals were saying because they hadn't invented writing yet. So these drawings could have been done not by a primitive Picasso, but by a youthful Gary Larson instead.

Ashley Montague, in his wonderful book *Growing Young,* points out that there are three biologic processes given by God and evolution to help us cope with stress. These help us meet the primary goal shared by most of us—"to die young—as late as possible." We all want to live long, but feel young and healthy as long as we can. The three processes are yawning, crying and laughing. They each share the same curve of biologic response. A person starts with a given amount of stress, the tension temporarily increases during these processes and then the tension is dissipated. The person ends up with less stress after these brief experiences.

I followed Ashley at a conference in Princeton and pointed out that I thought he had omitted at least one process with the same physiology—the human sexual response cycle. For any of you who may have experienced a sexual response cycle or two, or who can remember back to those thrilling days of yesteryear, or who can imagine along if you haven't made the trip yet, you may be aware that you are more relaxed after the sex (unless your in-laws are sleeping the the next room).

It also occurred to me immediately that you could probably get really relaxed if you could get all four of those responses in the same sitting—laughing, yawning, crying and sex. I think that's actually how they came up with the term "mellow" in Marin County, California, in the first place. But as a physician, I must warn you that the sequence is very important. If you start with the yawn, you could get to crying, but you probably wouldn't find your partner too interested in making the whole trip.

"Laughter can't heal a broken leg," says comedian Sid Ceasar, "but it can put you in a frame of mind to feel better faster." People who laugh may find their pain threshold increased. And I am convinced that folks who use laughter more often will be up and around more quickly after that broken leg. There is also a tantalizing bit of early research which suggests that laughing helps your immune system to fight disease. All this will need more study but it is a little hard to get the Reagan White House to fund good humor research, possibly because the researchers might use some of the Reagan years as a source of humor. (I urge you to consult the scholarly and hilarious book by Art Buchwald about the Reagan years called *I Don't Think I Remember*.)

It seems to me that the positive physiology of laughter lasts for a period of time *after* the laughter stops. A good Woody Allen movie makes me feel good, more resilient and in a better frame of mind for about a day. A Gary Larson cartoon or a Dave Barry column may last several hours—if you take two, you won't have to call me in the morning. I call this the "Humor Half-Life"—the time it takes for about half the beneficial effects of anything funny to wear off.

This is very similar to our use of medications. We give another dose of a drug when half the effects of the last dose wear off. It's not an accident that aspirin is taken every four hours; that's when half of the drug is gone.

So I suggest that you try to tune in to your own Humor Half-Life after any amount of silliness. Give yourself another "dose" of funniness as soon as you need to. It's important to do this throughout the day at work, at home and at play. You will feel more refreshed, more creative and will be a heck of a lot more fun to be around

Your own "Funnybone" will be unique. No one else has to think what you think is funny is funny for them—unless you are trying to make a living as a humorist. Then at least a few of your audience should have grinned on more than one occasion.

I encourage you to use your natural silliness creatively. To use silliness to its fullest, you have to understand the origin of the word. It has come to mean "inane" and "stupid"—the worst of childishness. And yet "silly" comes from the Middle English word "selig." Three hundred hears ago "selig" meant four things—"blessed," "prosperous," "happy," and "healthy." And to my mind, them's what we are all striving to achieve in life.

Along with the folks in this book, I urge you to get downright silly as quickly as possible and stay that way!

En-Joy!

Photo Credit: Al Francekevich Photography 73, New York

Dr. Allen's "No Fail" Juggling Stress Break

Take three square scarves—preferably of floaty, lightweight nylon—and get into the spirit by holding, tossing, waving and dropping them without apology (Dr. Allen's "guilt-free drop")

• *The Single Cross-Toss:* Pinch one scarf, palm down, in the center. Toss it high by throwing your arm across your body, then releasing the scarf. Catch it with the other hand, palm down. Now cross-toss and catch, starting with the opposite hand.

• *The Exchange:* Hold a scarf in each hand, palm down. Throw the right-hand scarf first, then keeping your eye on it, toss the second. Catch each scarf with the hand opposite the one that threw it.

• *The Jug:* Take two scarves in your right hand, one in palm and pinky, the second between thumb and forefinger. Hold the third in your left hand. Toss the thumb-and-forefinger right-hander first. Focusing on it, throw the scarf in your left hand, then use that hand to catch the first-thrown scarf. Throw the third (from your right hand), catching the second scarf in your right hand. Catch the third in your left.

• *Juggling:* Your aim: keeping a scarf airborne. That means tossing the first scarf before catching the third in "The Jug," and continuously tossing the next whenever one scarf is high. Along the way, you'll probably laugh and squeal and feel good—the best Rx for Stress.

Herb True, Ph.D.
1717 E. Colfax
South Bend, IN 46617
(219) 234-2340

Herb True

Who's Herb? Herb Who? Herb True! What does he know about "Funny Bones"? Herb True is a professional funny bone whacker.

Dr. Herb True is the "World's Greatest Edu-tainer. He is a provocative, witty, inspiring and informative platform speaker who averages135 presentations a year on motivation, creativity, selling, management, and the psychology of humor.

Dr. True travels around the world whacking peoples' funny bones. When they have their guards down, he zaps them with profound truths that often change their lives for the better. He is that rare combination of Entertainer/Educator. Dr. True has presented his custom built programs to over 4,100 groups. Herb says he has a "B.A., M.A., a Ph.D. and a note from his mother." He is the Adjunct Professor of Management, Department of Management, at the University of Notre Dame College of Business Administration, and has lectured at 50 other universities. Dr. True's philosophy is summed up in his own famous quotation,

"Anyone can count the seeds in an apple,
But who can count the apples in one seed?"

Dr. True's Team International has recently produced "Dr. True's own Humor Library," by topic, on computer database. Ideal for all speakers, it eliminates the "where do I put it-how do I find it" blues. A perfect tool to help speakers store, find and structure information for programs, workshops, articles, book and audio manuscripts. Distributed by the American Humor Guild, 1717 Colfax, South Bend, IN 46617, (219) 234-2340.

Introduction

By Herb True

"A merry heart doeth good like a medicine."
- Solomon

Humor Power
Is Humor A Special Spiritual Force?

"God must have meant for us to laugh, or He wouldn't have made so many mules, parrots, monkeys and human beings." - Abraham Lincoln

The sacred power of humor can be used by you and me as a common, though certainly not ordinary, part of our lives because it's God's medium.

That idea may shock some people and surprise others. To the shocked, it may seem sacrilegious to think of Yahweh, or Creator, as one who utilizes a need to use the power of humor. To the surprised, it may seem merely incredible! What—humor in the Bible? Humor as part of our Judeo-Christian heritage? Humor a power to help us cope and communicate in the true spirit of Christianity? Both the shocked and the surprised may have trouble accepting the fact of Godly humor.

Yet the New Testament reveals that Jesus told humorous stories (we may call them parables) and topped them with numerous punch lines. Jesus used satire, irony, wry wit, and he made repeated references to the need for a childlike spirit.

God, it seems clear, intended for each of us to develop our humor power because our Father knew words alone would be inadequate. He added to humanity's expressions, smiles and laughs. Then to make sure we took the hint to "think funny," God created the duckbill platypus, elephants, anteaters and other humorous animals.

Helen Salsbury made the same thought live in a poem that has become part of the lore of humor. "Who watches the ostrich swallow, then doubts that God likes to play?"

It seems unlikely that a perfectly staid, ever-serious Creator could ever have imagined mankind! Even after we recognize that God showed humor power by striping the zebra and stretching out the giraffe, the idea of humor in the Bible may still appear strange to the Purist.

Humor & Comedy

Our tendency to confuse humor and comedy might explain some of this. Biblical humor as opposed to comedy doesn't provide the same kind of yaks and belly laughs. Comedy is banana peel burlesque. Comedy makes people laugh. Comedians evaluate how good they are by how much people laugh—how long, how many times, etc. Much of comedy laughter is caused by embarrassment.

Humor is often subtle, relying on intellectual playfulness, although it also appeals to the emotions, especially in the New Testament. Humor lifts the load, relieves anxiety. The main difference I think is that humor's purpose is to help you laugh "with" rather than "at" people, to make events memorable, to reflect on our spiritual goodness without becoming vain and self-centered.

The Old Testament statement, "Even in laughter, the heart is sorrowful," reminds us that comedy and laughter alone are inadequate to alleviate pain. Exactly because life is serious, we need the vast, helpful nonthreatening energy generated by humor power.

In both the Old and New Testaments, some evidence of God's humor power is beyond our comprehension. Our finite minds often miss the infinite points. But that isn't always the fault of our understanding nor is it usually caused by too much subtlety. The many examples of hearty humor in the form of puns and other plays on words, exist in the Bible but usually open their full energy only to those scholars capable of reading the Hebrew of the Old Testament and the Greek of the New. The stress releasing and learning power of word related humor doesn't often translate well from one language to another.

Decoding the Texts

The various English translations of the Bible offer innumerable examples of God's mirth, but the very familiarity of Biblical verses could prevent us from seeing their intended humor. If we can put Bible stories into modern language—"slanguage" it might help us to get the point.

Some Biblical humor comes through to us with little need for intepretationw. For example: The humor power of Proverbs relates closely to modern one-liners. Example: "As snow in summer, and as rain in harvest, so honour is not seemly for a fool."

Unlike comedy, the humor appreciaton of Proverbs doesn't call forth hearty laugher. The thought of snow in summer, rain in harvest leads to a humor-powered, surprising comparison—honor for a fool.

Then consider "The glory of young men is in their strength; and the beauty of old men is the grey beard." These and other Proverbs gently suggest the power of humor—gently, but with a "think funny" twist or jolt.

In our leading quotation, "A merry heart doeth good like a medicine," the wisdom of Solomon anticipated modern medical science, which with the help of Norman Cousins, has discovered the medicinal powers of humor. As the rest of that Proverb says, "A broken spirit drieth the bones."

Be Joyful

Pertinent Proverbs demonstrate Biblical humor. The book of Psalms stresses the importance of gladness, joy and even playfulness. Psalm 100 was a favorite of Jesus. "Make a joyful noise unto the Lord, all ye lands. Serve the Lord with gladness and come before His presence with singing." The idea of showing gladness by making a joyful noise and singing appears frequently. It is symbolic and metaphorical. We can make a joyful noise by showing the gladness and merriment in our own hearts.

The Old Testament offers powerful instances of humor in impossible situations. Perhaps most familiar is the story of suffering in the Book of Job. We speak of the patience of Job, but he was a highly impatient man who could bear his trials only with the help of ironical wit.

"No doubt but ye are the people, and wisdom shall die with you," says Job and later, "I have heard many such things: miserable comforters are ye all."

Can we doubt that he was, ironically, mocking his critics for their smug belief that they were "all knowing?" His second comment changes readily into modern terms: "No way! Don't tell me your sad stories. I've got troubles enough already."

"The Fight On the Cliff..."

Other stories from the Old Testament illustrate humor power with the chill of suspense, and the amusing thrill of the unexpected in the happy ending. Consider the story of Joseph, who was the victim of what we would now call "sibling rivalry." It opens with grimness, for this brothers resented Joseph's coat of many colors, given by their father to his favorite son. They were angered by Joseph's dreams of glory.

After ponderous planning and plotting, the brothers waited by the pit in Dothan. As Joseph neared it, one brother said sarcastically, "Behold, the dreamer cometh."

Here again modern terms might reveal humor power: "Hey! That dreamy kid just made the scene." The brothers put Joseph into the pit and put their heads together. "We will say some evil beast hath devoured him. Then we shall see what will become of his dreams."

The brothers' second thoughts saved Joseph. They recoiled from the ultimate crime of his death, and preferred to sell him into Egypt for "twenty pieces of silver." They cast their brother into a pit, but—on second thought—released him.

Because Joseph enjoyed the happy ending of becoming governor of Egypt, forgiving his brothers and being merry with them, we can enjoy the humor in the story. Joseph's many-colored coat may have been somewhat ludicrous, but his brothers behaved ridiculously, as well as cruelly.

Joseph's success and forgiving nature were energized with humor power. He was later able to be merry with his brothers.

We Love the Underdog

Suspenseful and lightly humorous, too, is the even more familiar story of David. A comparison of "unequals" turns on humor. In Samuel I we learn that Goliath was mighty and tall—six cubits, or six times 18 inches, plus a span, probably about nine inches. David's height isn't specified, but we know that he was "but a youth, ruddy and of a fair countenance." So we think of him as "little David."

In the battle with Goliath, David kept his armor, but discarded his sword in favor of five smooth stones and a slingshot. Doesn't that seem ludicrous and ridiculous? God's humor must have powered his sling, for one smooth stone was enough to conquer mighty, tall Goliath.

Humor Loosens Tension

Samuel I tells us that David returned to his tent and left his armor there. We can infer that he also unslung his "sling." He unslung his slingshot to sing gladly and make a joyful noise, in the Book of Psalms. Biblical scholars and writers frequently mention the need to "unstring your bow." This is no coincidence, but relates directly to David and his power to relax after his successful but grueling experience. A Boston minister in early American days wrote in "The Government and Improvement of Mirth" that "It spoils the bow to keep it always bent."

Long before that an Egyptian King explained, "In battle an archer strings his bow until it is taut. Later, he unstrings it. If he didn't it wouldn't be any good when he next needed it—no elasticity, no snap." All of us can benefit by snapping back from serious situations with relaxed humor power.

Perhaps our best example of the Divine power released when "the bow is unstrung" comes from Jesus. Some are inclined to think of him as sad and sorrowful. But today when we speak jokingly of "the blind leading the blind," "casting pearls before swine," "wolves in sheep's clothing," all without "stopping to think," all of these humorous images were first given to us by Jesus, who also said, "Ye blind guides, who strain at a gnat and swallow a camel."

We know from the life of Jesus, and the Bible, that humor power is often misunderstood, confused with comedy, and can't always be explained easily. But we know, too, that it is God's power, and ours to use. We can learn to generate humor power by considering how others have used it to lift loads and lighten burdens.

True Life Directions
CIRCA 1990

by Dr. Herb True

God does not expect great things from us.
God expects love from us.
Trusting in God with all my heart,
And leaning not on my own understanding,
I will in all my ways acknowledge Yahweh.
I am valuable because I was created
with an inner worth.
I do not have to nurture and protect my worth
from getting jaded or twisted by the temptations
of a success-at-any-cost oriented society.
If I can avoid the temptation
to possess secular success,
and adorn myself with accolades
at the expense of others,
I can create an environment of mutual trust.
A trust that says:
"I am valuable as you are valuable.
Let's make a value pact.
I will give you the best I have,
and I feel confident
that you will give me your best in return."

Laughter Keeps Them Young

BOB HOPE, 85

"Without laughter I would never have lived this long. All any one needs to keep a youthful interior and exterior is three good laughs a day."

GEORGE BURNS, 92

"I've always believed that life is a lot easier—and more fun—if you can laugh at yourself. Laughter has kept me young."

MILTON BERLE, 80

"Laughter keeps you young because it's better than the best prescriptions doctors can give you. Laughter releases the stress in your body. If people laughed more, they'd need doctors less and stay younger.

DANNY THOMAS, 74
"Anytime I'm feeling old and down, I use laughter like a prescription drug. Laughter can conquer anything—fear, illness, loneliness and especially old age!"

HENNY YOUNGMAN, 82
"Hearing people laugh at my jokes is the best medicine and is like a source of youth for me. It's free, plentiful and keeps me feeling like a million bucks!"

JIM BACKUS, 73
"Laughter has definitely helped me live to a ripe old age. Whenever I hear of a distressing situation, I try to find an angle on it where I can see a laugh."

Dr. Tom F.Steiner
Mary Jo Crowley Steiner
427 Jolina Way
Encinitas, CA 92024
(619) 942-8366 (619) 436-5835

Dr. Tom Steiner

Dr. Tom Steiner, the noted EnterTRAINer, has been on the professional speakers and trainers circuit for more than 10 years. He makes more than 250 presentations a year in addition to periodic appearances at local Comedy and Magic clubs.

His unique, fast paced style often includes clean comedy and magic to encourage option thinking. He attributes his sense of humor to growing up in New York City, where everyone is a comedian.

Mary Jo Crowley Steiner

Mary Jo Crowley Steiner is a stand-up comic who has performed at The Comedy Store and The Improvisation since 1982. She won the National Academy of Television Arts and Sciences "Emmy 1985 Comedy Challenge" and the Gold Medal at the Comedy Olympics in Los Angeles in 1986 and 1988.

She specializes in clean, custom comedy for corporate meetings and conventions. She attributes her sense of humor to being born in Cleveland.

The Power of Humor

By Dr. Tom Steiner and Mary Jo Crowley Steiner

"When the going gets weird, the weird turn professional."
- Dr. Hunter S. Thompson

As the first family of comedy in San Diego, we are on a mission to bring a smile to every face with a mouth on it. We want YOU to join us in this quest. But first, a little bit about who we are and what we've already done...

Appropriately, we met on April Fool's Day in

1986. I was doing a stand-up routine for the San Diego Museum of Art and Tom was the M.C. So every April Fool's Day, we celebrate the anniversary of our first meeting by demonstrating the "Power of Humor" in unusual places.

In 1987, we entertained at a convalescent home for patients, staff and families. The running joke that day was the patients had a choice for the evening—comedy or pain medication. (Of course, they didn't have to choose, but only one-quarter of the typical amount of pain medications were given out that night.)

We wore oversized white lab coats, antennas, funny hats and did hospital humor. Some of it was slapstick ("The Mayo Clinic is on the phone." "Put them on hold." "You want me to hold the Mayo?").

A year later, on April Fool's Day, 1988, we received permission to tell jokes to people in line at the Unemployment Office in San Diego. It took us two years to convince the manager that the clients wouldn't tar and feather us.

Imagine the following scene: Every time an unhappy camper walked up to the counter, the staff would begin snapping their fingers and strutting a little Motown two-step. Then they would sing 30 seconds of the oldie, "Get A Job." Not one of the unemployed waiting in line thought this was designed to make fun of them. They realized that the situation called for a relief from the sadness. It humanized an otherwise impersonal situation.

Smile-A-Day

Humor makes sense. It encourages people to view the world with optimism and joy. It is the bedrock of mental health in that happy people find reasons to smile when others are gloomy. In the business world, humor make cents too. It establishes instant rapport and warm bonds between co-workers. It even soothes grumpy customers.

We conspicuously try to use humor to brighten our own lives as well as to enliven the people we see each day. It is our sincere hope that YOU, too, will join us in this "Smile - A - Day" crusade.

It has long been recognized that humor has many benefits in terms of physical health. There is no doubt that laughter affects the brain. (Look at us!) Laughter stimulates the production of catecholamines, which release natural pain killers called endorphins. You can produce your own endorphins or you can see them perform with the whales at Sea World.

When a person laughs, the lungs expand, the arteries dilate, the body temperature rises and the endocrine system is stimulated. So it's good exercise, as well. In fact, we are hoping laughter becomes a recognized field of medicine because we already have matching Cadillacs picked out.

Find the Fun

Humor has equal value in dealing with mental health. When individuals become angry, depressed, anxious, or just fatigued, their thought processes become quite restricted. Most people in this "hopeless and hapless" mode think in terms of only two options. This dichotomous logic (or black and white thinking) tends to restrict their options in thought and action. Humor can help. In order to be funny or create a joke, the individual must look at something in the world and then find a way to twist, stretch or change an element of the situation. This is exactly what creates the joke. It is this process which also allows the person to find a way out of the difficult situation. Finding the funny part may represent one more option for the person to use to cope with the situation. If a person is willing to deal with the trauma with this expanded view, he has the ability to begin to see "a way out."

Father Joe Carroll, who runs the St. Vincent de Paul Center for the Homeless in San Diego, reports that on a food line one Friday, a fellow looked at the meal, looked at Father Joe, and said "Filet Mignon, again ?!" Being able to smile while in this line may help the person to see value in himself and in his situation.

Being funny is a perfect defense against feeling overwhelmed. The knowledge that we have resources within ourselves to convert difficult situations to more comical situations is a wondrous ally. Standing in line at a restaurant only to be greeted by a mindless hostess, asking, "Would you care to be seated now?" becomes a lot more palatable when you respond, "No, we'd prefer to stand on a balance beam while we eat dinner." Telling the waiter that you will be his customer tonight, before he can tell you that he will be your waiter tonight, gives you the upper hand in the upcoming dinner negotiations. You can also enjoy a startled reaction from a waiter if you know the dinner specials, and can recite them to him flawlessly. At the end of the meal, ask if he takes Hawaiian money. We always get a kick out of how many waiters say "No."

My sister is a waitress who enjoys good banter with her dinner customers. One night her auto mechanic showed up, and she did what all of us would love to do. She gave him a bill for $347. Shocked, he insisted, "This is outrageous! That's not what the prices on the menu said." She replied, "The prices on the menu are only ESTIMATES of what it costs to eat here !"

Diffuse Anger with Humor

Volatile emotions, such as anger, can also be diminished by using humor. When speaking to married couples, I remind them that the next time they are fighting in round number 463, (that's where within three minutes you have no idea what you are fighting about, but she's just called your mother a hamster) doing something humorous might change the tempo of the interaction. I always encourage one of the spouses to take off all of their clothes immediately and continue to argue with their body parts jingling and jangling around. If he is still angry, I suggest that the wife say, "I can see that point you are trying to make, but I've got two of my own." It is not the nudity that will stop the fight. That will only work twice. (Once because one spouse will say, "I can't believe you did that." And it'll work one more time because one spouse will say, "I can't believe you did that AGAIN!")

The reason the fight will stop, involves changing the options available to the combatants at the moment. Now they can choose whether to think about the good things in their relationship or what they are presently arguing about. We can give our personal guarantee as to the positive effects of this tactic, since we use it all of the time. Like most couples, we argue about only three things: Money, sex and Frank Sinatra ("I want it MY way").

In a recent lecture about anger, I reminded the audience that animals are much smarter than humans in the way they fight. Rattlesnakes will wind around each other and the winner is the one who winds up on top. The losing snake just slinks away. Rhinoceri, or many animals of the rhinocerous persuasion, batter their horns against each other as opposed to goring and maiming each other in the flank. My favorite example is the kissing fish. They simply lock lips and push. The loser is the one who gets pushed backwards, but there are worse ways of having to give in. Imagine couples trying this tactic as a way of diffusing anger.

I once was introduced to a bank branch manager with a very bad temper. He would not hesitate to get up and charge across the bank to reprimand an employee without thinking about the impact on the employee or his peers, not to mention the customers. When asked about it, he said it was just his quick temper. I suggested that he keep a pair of swim fins in his bottom desk drawer. Whenever the urge to throttle an employee would come over him, I suggested that he remove his shoes and put on the swim fins. Then he could try to cross the bank lobby, and still be angry (and upright) by the time he got across the bank. You can imagine that not only did he get a laugh out of his predicament, but he often softened his critique when he finally did arrive.

My mother knew how to change anger into laughter, and use it to her advantage. When my brother and I were little, we behaved as if we were a classic definition of "sibling rivalry." My mother used to punish us by making us clean windows, but there was one "catch": we had to wash the same window at the same time, with him on the outside and me on the inside.

Well, folks, it's not possible, when you're ages seven and nine, to wash a window and not make faces, stick out your tongue, wave your arms around, and eventually end up laughing like loons. Best of all, mom got all the windows cleaned.

Humor and Depression

Depression is another area where humor can be of great value. Most depressed individuals tend to generalize their concerns rapidly. What were once molehills are now the Himalayas. I used to teach a Personal Growth class entitled, "Enjoying Your Depression." The students came in with many different concerns. Among them were "professional victims," people who seemed to wander through life like an accident waiting to happen. I would try to get people to exchange their depressions by role playing each others' current crisis. Seeing another, somewhat exaggerated, view of their concerns would often help people to see that they were limiting their options. Therapists are reminded of Milton Erickson, who would confront patients with exaggerated caricatures of their symptoms. One chronic complainer was exasperated when Erickson cut off her whining about her ailing knee by saying, "Your knee, my whole leg." She insisted that she didn't want to sit there and listen to all of Erickson's problems. Letting the patient experience this allowed Erickson to make a breakthrough in showing her how she was responsible for many of the traumas of her life.

I used to visit a 72-year-old woman in an oncology ward. She was dying a slow and painful death from cancer, and I would visit her regularly to tell her jokes to get her to laugh. I would blacken out a tooth, put antennas on my head—basically anything for a laugh. One day she said to me, "You're the only one who cares whether I laugh again or not. Everyone else is too busy trying to keep me alive." With me she could die part-time, instead of full-time. My brief visits allowed her to appreciate the joy of still being able to laugh in her remaining months. Although she has long since died, her words still keep ringing in my ears.

Humor doesn't necessarily decline with age either. My 95-year-old aunt used to live in a Senior Citizen's Center in New York City (bet you didn't think New Yorkers lived to be 95). She would proudly walk around with a necklace that had a large, polished brown stone hanging from it. She would say to anyone who seemed interested in it, "This is a very expensive necklace. Do you know what kind of a stone this is ?" No one would dare guess that it was her largest and most recently removed gallstone. Now, that takes real gall.

Not to be outdone, a 96-year-old friend of hers would stuff large pillows up under the front of her dresses. She was known for walking over to males of any age and asking, "Are you the father of my baby ?" We can only hope to be that feisty in our 90's.

Workers of the Heart

Hospitals have a unique need for humor, as well. Medical professionals walk a tightrope, trying not to get too involved. For example, they will refer to the "heart patient in Room 204," instead of using the person's name. In hospital settings, humor can be used to distract a patient from his pain. When the nurse feels the teddy bear's forehead, and shows him a lot of attention, the young patient may forget about his own pain for a moment. While we don't believe humor is a cure-all, we sure believe it helps.

Companies could take a lesson from hospitals. They have an "Admitting Department." We imagine that means, whenever anything goes wrong, a whole bunch of people stand up and say, "Okay, okay, WE DID IT !!"

Humor keeps our sanity and insanity balanced and in perspective. It has been said that a sense of humor is an index of adjustment to one's environment, no matter how crazy it actually is. When confronted by a client with a multiple personality, I think about saying, "OK, which one of you has the insurance?" I can't help but want to bill the client with slight amnesia BEFORE we have our session. And I can't help wondering which closet the schizophrenic, transvestite will finally come out of.

Having worked as a therapist, teacher and crisis counselor, I know the energy drain associated with constantly trying to help others in need. I know there were days when I wanted to permanently pull all of my hair out and get a job grooming dogs or arranging flowers. I know that "workers of the heart" often burn-out before their time because it seems difficult and pointless to help in certain situations. In my work with the dying, suicidal and drugged-out clients, it was particularly necessary to be able to develop an attitude of "detached concern." This seeming oxymoron means giving 110% when working with the client, then being able to evaluate your work and let it go. Additionally, it is important to be able to refocus yourself on an energy enhancing activity. My comedy and magic career began as a way for me to hear the laughter again.

On Stage

Anxiety can also be relieved by using a sense of humor. In my first attempt at comedy, I invited 150 of my closest friends to attend my debut. I instructed each of them to bring a rose and an egg and then decide which one to throw at me after the show. Within the first three minutes, it was getting increasingly clear that I had entered "Comedy Hell," where no one laughs at anything. Joke after joke failed and the sight gags did worse. My anxiety was getting to be overwhelming. Suddenly out of my mouth popped, "Hey, you know I have another job; I don't do comedy for a living." The audience and I both enjoyed this moment of relief from the silence. After the show, the audience was still not sure whether they had witnessed an act of incredible courage or a simple case of brain damage on stage. It took many more trips to the Comedy Store on Amateur Night before I was able to be funny for a living.

Humor at Work

Humor can be especially helpful to change the tempo and turn a situation around in the workplace. Before I began in the comedy field, I was a real estate writer. Even today, I am not always sure which is which. Humor used to come in handy when dealing with impatient builders. One day I met a real estate developer who was annoyed that his project was being delayed. Before he could begin to build, archeologists needed to examine the site to make sure it wasn't historically significant. He was impatient and wanted to build big, expensive homes right away. "What do they think they're going to find ?" he asked angrily. I said, "Relax. Maybe they'll find a $20,000 house."

Another use of humor in the workplace is to break up the monotony of daily routines. A receptionist reports she cracked up when a caller left this message for her boss: "Tell him Mr. Wolfman called. As in, Frankenstein meets..." She also notes another man called, and his surname was Czerniejewski. She asked, "Sir, how do you spell that?" His reply: "Just like it sounds."

I used to work at a company where I thought of my boss as a father figure. That really irritated her. She should have known I had a sense of humor when she interviewed me for the position. She asked, "What would you like to be doing in five years and what are you doing right now to get there?" I replied, "I want YOUR job. And I've poisoned your coffee."

Though they may have to rent a personality, even engineers can have a sense of humor. One electronics company in Southern California has a dog on its Board of Directors. At meetings, the dog sits on a chair and has full voting rights. Indeed, it has been argued on occasion that the dog was the most intelligent one at the meeting.

Another high tech company in San Diego has a group of engineers who are working on a classified government project. The box contains four component boards, which they have named after ducks—Hewey, Dewey, Screwey and Louie. These engineers convinced their project manager to spring for $200 to purchase duck insignias for their lab coats.

Another defense contractor—and this will make you sleep better at night—has named its computers "Bert" and "Ernie," after the Sesame Street characters.

We also believe that humor has a place in advertising. Suppose the United States Postal Service came out with an ad campaign that used the slogan, "Reach

Out and Lick Someone." Suppose the utility company in your city started using the slogan, "We Look Into Your Shorts" on the side of its repair vehicles.

I recently saw a radiator repair company with "The Best Place in Town to Take a Leak" printed on the sides on its vehicles. I'm sure a handkerchief manufacturer has used "Put Your Nose in Our Business." Amtrak could use, "Let us run YOU out of town on a rail."

Finding humor in your life or in your work doesn't necessarily mean walking around with a Groucho Marx nose and glasses face or wearing antennas, although it can be fun to do so. It means anything, however subtle, that can bring a smile to you or someone else.

A few examples of how to find humor in the medical environment are:

• One dentist wears a mask when he or a patient has a cold, and draws a nose and big whiskers on the mask.

• One doctor likes to take the thermometer out of his patient's mouth, and remark, "You're about a quart low."

• One EKG (electrocardiograph) technician enjoys rolling up the long tape, while telling the patient, "When the doctor is done looking at this, we'll have a ticker tape parade."

A few things you might try include:

• Leave funny messages for people. Tell someone he had a call from the President of the United States, area code 202 (make up a seven digit number ending in 000).

• Leave a rubber fish in the water cooler. Or, in California, we suggest several olives and a swizzle stick.

• When entering an elevator, always stand facing one of the rear corners. For effect, scratch at your chin thoughtfully. When the elevator door opens up, leave and simultaneously scream, "It happened again !!"

• During slow periods, we recommend hooking all paper clips together or stapling all items to the desk.

• Gluing money to the floor in high traffic areas brings out the best in people, as well.

• Attaching plastic faucets, wind-up motors and switchplates (with the suction cup backings) in unusual locations typically get noticed.

• Carry a magic wand (clear plexiglass is nice) with you to use when the boss wants something done yesterday. Wave the wand over your desk, while howling some "secret words" of your own concoction. (If something occurs, let us know; we will be happy to market your product with you.) If nothing occurs, start asking everyone around you for the the number of the wand repair company, while screaming that you can't do magic without the proper equipment.

• Keep a bright red fire hat and a noisy siren in your desk for your boss' next fire drill. Be careful. In some companies, if you don't drill you get fired. You'll know if you work for this kind of company if your boss' management style is Management By Rambo.

• One of our personal favorites involves bringing a bullhorn to work with you. Stand outside an engineering lab, turn the volume up to 7, and in a stern voice state, "Engineers, we have the lab surrounded. Come out with your calculators up."

We do have one caution for you to observe. ALWAYS make sure that the person receiving the humorous gesture will appreciate it, particularly if your victim is your BOSS !! Remember Rule Number One in our course is, Keep Your Job !! Rule Number Two is, Remember Rule Number One. Rule Number Three is Never Pull a Practical Joke on Anyone With Access To Your Personnel File.

The Sweetest Sound

We hope that we have convinced you to join us in the Smile-A-Day crusade. Imagine how different your life might be if you found a way to smile every day and got others to join in !! While we can't guarantee you a comedy career, we can guarantee you a lot of laughs. Laughter is the sweetest sound we've ever heard. Take two punchlines and call us in the morning!!

Join us and start laughing today!!

Photo Credit & ©: Tom Priest Photography, Carlsbad, CA

Thoughts on Health & Humor

"A sense of humor keen enough to show a man his own absurdities will keep him from the commission of all sins, or nearly all, save those that are worth committing."
- Samuel Butler the Younger

"No sky is heavy if the heart be light."
- Winston Churchill

The essence of humor is sensibility; warm tender fellow-feeling with all forms of existence.
- Carlyle

Your Thoughts on Health & Humor

Gary Screaton Page, M.Ed.
The Achievers
117 Northwood Drive
Welland, Ontario, Canada
L3C 6S4
1-416-734-4280

REGISTERED AMERICAN ENTREPRENEURS' ASSOCIATION MEMBER

THE ACHIEVERS
HOME TUTORING SERVICE

Gary Screaton Page

Gary Screaton Page has been married to his wife, Rotraud, for twenty-three years. They have a daughter, Deidre, and a son, Jason. Gary received his B.A. from York University and his M.Ed. from the University of Toronto. Currently, Gary is completing his Ed.D. in Education Psychology.

Gary Page has taught all levels from grade one through university, during his twenty-five years as a teacher. Co-author of Personalized Parenting: Be the Parent You Want to Be, *Gary has published more than a dozen articles on a wide range of education issues, and was a Contributing Editor of* The Educational Courier *magazine for five years. For eight years he was a Professional Development Instructor for the Ontario Public School Teachers' Federation which, in August, 1979, awarded him the $10,000 Win Davies Memorial Scholarship for outstanding ability and scholarly achievement in education.*

He has appeared on Canada A.M., Hour Long, *and* Take Thirty, *spoken at many education conferences and hosted a documentary mini-series entitled* What Did You Do In School Today? *for CHEX TV in Peterborough, Ontario. He was an education consultant for CHEX TV'S children's show* The Silver Basketball.

Gary is the Assistant Pastor at First Baptist Church, teaches English at Thorold Secondary School and is Director of THE ACHIEVERS Home Tutoring Service in Welland, Ontario.

Laughter Is the Best Medicine

By Gary Screaton Page

"True humor springs not more from the head than from the heart; it is not contempt, its essence is love; it issues not in laughter but in still smiles, which lie far deeper."
—Thomas Carlyle

Sunday morning began more peacefully than Saturday evening ended. All was quiet on the home front. The war had ended. Rotraud, my wife, and our two children slept soundly upstairs. I alone was awake. The solitude gave me time to reflect upon our heated discussion of the night before. Disagreements occur in every family, including ours. However, we end confrontation with a powerful weapon. Humor regularly paves the way to peace and reconciliation among us. An intense and driven crew, we know a sense of humor can calm life's troubled waters.

Humor Paves the Way to Peace

Fortunately, one doesn't have to be a stand-up comic to use humor effectively. I learned long ago that a sense of humor can be cultivated and I've tried to teach my children that they, too, can develop a light-hearted approach to everyday annoyances. A sense of playfulness best characterizes a sense of humor. The animated face, the twinkling eye, the bounce in one's step all show an upbeat approach to life. Mirth, not worth makes our family rich.

That Sunday morning humor added to our family's treasure chest. Knowing that the best way to a kid's heart is through the stomach, I made a breakfast none of us would ever forget. Pancakes! But, not just any run-of-the-mill pancakes. I made the lightest pancakes the children had ever seen!

"Come and get'm," I called when all was ready. "Come and get the lightest pancakes you've ever eaten."

One by one the three sleepy heads appeared in the dining room. There, carefully hung by thread from the chandelier, three pancakes floated over each plate. "The pancakes were so light," I quipped, "I couldn't keep them on your plates." Laughter filled the room. Peace reigned again.

He Who Laughs Lasts

Laughter lifts. He who laughs lasts. A joke told at the right moment, the comic twist in an otherwise embarrassing moment, and even the lowly pun have transformed even my most difficult situations. But, to make humor work I've taken the risks inherent in dealing playfully with difficult situations. Developing a sense of humor demanded I become less self-centered and more other-oriented. To recognize signs of tension in myself and others and to respond reflexively with humor has taken practice and conscious effort. Fortunately, the rewards for dealing lightheartedly with life have far outweighed the risks. The person with a sense of humor will almost always win the day.

Three Principles of Humor

And, even the risks can be minimized. Three principles guide my use of humor in difficult situations: anxiety is the root of all humor; some things are too serious to joke about; never have fun at another's expense.

1. Anxiety in Humor

First, I recognize that all humor has some level of anxiety at its root. We all laugh at the circus clown's pratfalls, or the antics of Keaton's tramp because laughter eases the tension created by the pathos of the characters. We've all been clumsy and fallen down; we've all been the brunt of the bully at some time. Such serious circumstances create tension. Humor and laughter relieve it. The potential injury to the falling clown causes stress; but, his rising uninjured and undaunted releases our anxiety. The unexpected turn of events—the twist of fate—makes us laugh and we relax again.

In a joke, the punchline makes us laugh. The story line, usually tied to some serious subject matter, builds tension. Then, the otherwise realistic, logical and reasonable story does an about face around an absurd incongruity that makes us laugh. The story builds tension in us and the punchline releases the tension through our laughter. Whatever the source, an absurd visual image, a story or a play on words, it's still the unexpected twist that makes us laugh and relieves the tension.

Every job has stressful moments. As a high school teacher, and as a Pastor, I meet them daily. I've learned, however, that at work, as at home, finding the positive, lighthearted side of an otherwise negative situation reduces the stress. For example, when teaching in a large elementary school several years ago, I found myself at a staff meeting defending an unpopular administrative policy. I spoke at length supporting the rationale for the new direction. My remarks reached their climax and ended on a note of optimism that the new policy would work to the advantage of all. When I sat down, I leaned forward more than I should have and struck my head on the conference table. Tension filled the air as those present strained to contain their laughter. Quickly, I regained my composure, stood up and boldly added, "Knock wood!"

The phrase, to be sure, was old and worn out. Yet, at that moment, on that occasion, the remark proved refreshing. It eased the tension and allowed us to move on. My awkward moments prove fertile ground for sowing humor.

Unfortunately, one can make people too tense or too anxious. Or, they may feel too little tension. In either case they will see no humor in a situation or story. Our attempt to be humorous will fall flat. We may even offend. To fully appreciate a joke requires a delicate balance between too little and too much anxiety.

Whether people respond well to my efforts to relieve tension with humor in specific situations, depends upon how those people relate to the circumstances. If they experience too little anxiety, they'll not be amused. If they identify too strongly, their anxiety grows and I'll "bomb."

2. Some Things Too Serious To Joke About

My second consideration when using humor, then, is to recognize that some things are too serious to joke about. Some jokes may be too crude or tasteless to be amusing. The so-called "hate jokes," popular in the fifties, have fortunately passed from the scene. And, ordinarily, one still doesn't crack jokes at funerals.

Yet, even on these solemn occasions I've found that a sense of humor can ease the pain. As Assistant Pastor of the church I attend, I conducted a former member's funeral service. The deceased was known for her sense of humor. So, in the eulogy I told one of her favorite stories. I confess, I wasn't sure that I should; after all, we Baptists tend to be a conservative lot, and funerals are sad and solemn occasions. I wasn't completely certain that laughter was appropriate. Nevertheless, moved by the Spirit, I related the following:

One morning, when waiting for the laboratory technician to come and take a sample of her blood, Margaret sat dressed in the usual hospital gown. Adorning her head, though, was not the usual hospital cap. Rather, a kerchief-like chapeau covered her hair. The ends of the knots which secured her "hat" extended like two long floppy ears, one on each side of her head.

Arriving on the scene the laboratory technician looked at Margaret. "Oh, this is wonderful," he grinned, "my first 'rabbit test'."

At that point the mourners, including the deceased woman's family, laughed openly. The rest of the service proceeded in the traditional fashion. Later, over lunch, which followed the funeral, the woman's son expressed his appreciation. "Mother loved a good laugh," he said, "She'd be happy you told that story."

Our laughter proved a fitting tribute to a woman who had touched so many lives with her sense of humor.

3. Avoid Sarcasm

My last consideration is to avoid sarcasm when I use humor to ease tension or avoid confrontation. Long ago one of my high school teachers showed me humor's tasteless and hurtful side. He taught me first-hand that nothing alienates another faster than sarcasm. Humor at the expense of others isn't funny.

Mr. Smith (the name has been changed to protect the guilty) was a master at cutting remarks. One day I mistakenly told him about a new method I was trying to learn in the hopes of improving my skill in spelling. I really tried to learn the method, and even raised my spelling grade by fifteen per cent.

Unfortunately, when report cards came out I still failed. With each report he handed to its owner, Mr. Smith made a comment. As he handed me mine I waited to hear what he would say. "That new spelling technique of yours, Page, it's clearly a winner. You only failed by eight per cent!" he declared sarcastically, "Maybe you could teach us all how to use it."

Everyone laughed but me. I couldn't. I was too hurt and embarrassed. After class, however, several classmates panned Mr.Smith's comic performance. As it turned out he'd lost more than me that day. When he took his shot at me, even though he got his laugh, the other students knew he could get them, too. No one wants to live in fear of being the next victim of the cheap shot—funny or not. Sarcasm turns people off, not on. A joke, to be appropriate, must be appreciated by everyone, not just the joker.

Using Humor Effectively

Happily, some sensitive teachers, who used humor more effectively, came into my life. Mr. MacFarlane was one such teacher. He always had a story to settle us down just before we left the classroom. I've forgotten most of them now; but, one I'll never forget.

Opening our study of the early North American fur traders, Mr. MacFarlane explained how the Nor'Westers had trapped and hunted. Face as straight as you please, he concluded the lesson with the following:

"You know," he began, "like the Nor'Westers, I like hunting. I've hunted for years. But, hunting can be dangerous. I remember one winter hunting trip I went on with my father. He'd just taught me to fire his old flint-lock rifle and I was eager to try my luck in the woods.

"We trekked in for about an hour," Mr. MacFarlane continued. "As we did, I somehow got separated from my father. I began to call out as I searched for him. I backtracked, unaware I was being followed. Close behind me was a large black bear. Closer and closer it came. Suddenly, I turned. The bear growled menacingly and I ran as fast as my legs would carry me. But, the bear ran even faster and gained quickly.

"The frozen snow crunched under my racing feet as the bear drew close behind. In spite of the cold," he declared dryly, "I sweated so badly, the perspiration ran out my coat sleeve into my flint-lock. Soon the sweat froze and ice plugged the rifle muzzle.

"The bear kept gaining. But, I managed to keep ahead—until I tripped on a dead branch. I fell hard to the ground. The bear came closer. I knew if I didn't shoot him then, I'd be his next meal.

"Fortunately, I'd already loaded the powder into the old flint-lock. Unfortunately, Dad had the pouch with the rifle balls. Worse, the frozen sweat still plugged the muzzle. In desperation I pulled the trigger anyway, hoping the noise would frighten the bear now rearing menacingly over my head.

"The powder flashed. A large icicle of frozen sweat blasted from the muzzle. The icicle caught the bear right between the eyes and he fell to the ground, dead.

"Later, at camp," Mr. MacFarlane boldly continued, "we cut the bear up and discovered what had killed him. Do you know what he died of?" he asked.

We waited for the answer.

"Water on the brain!" he declared, as seriously as when he had started his tall tale.

His were not the greatest jokes. But, they always came at the right time and I'll always remember him for them.

The Positive Side of Negative Situations

In the final analysis, then, a sense of humor is nothing more, or less, than the ability to look for the positive, light-hearted side of a negative situation—the comic slant. That comic twist can come from an unexpected and witty remark, a funny face, a playful wink, or a verbal surprise. The following incident will illustrate this.

One busy Saturday morning on my first job as parceller for a large chain of grocery stores, I nervously packed the area manager's order. He'd just completed his inspection of the store. I worked as I had never worked before, and packed every parcel just right. A large, fresh lettuce was the last item rung through the cash register. I picked it up quickly to wrap it before adding the lettuce to the sack. As I did, water, hidden among the leaves, sprayed out all over the superintendent's suit. At that moment I knew my career in the grocery business had ended.

Quickly I apologized. Then, I waited...

"Young man, you're fired!" I imagined Mr. McCormack's voice booming at me. But, that's not what happened.

"It's all right, son," he said smilingly, "Accidents happen. I'm impressed with how well you've been doing."

I couldn't believe my ears. "What a guy!" I thought to myself, "No wonder he's the boss!"

Mr. McCormack loaded the final sack into his shopping cart. As he wheeled his way toward the parking lot he looked back and quipped, "Remember, 'lettuce' not give everyone a shower my boy. This is a grocery business, not a bath house."

Some people say puns are the lowest form of humor. At that moment Mr. McCormack proved otherwise. He eased the tension and made me feel better. He also encouraged me with his compliment. There and then I determined to be the best grocery clerk he had in his territory. And, within four months of our meeting, I had worked my way up to the company's best paying part-time job. I became Captain of part-time help in Mr. McCormack's largest store.

It takes a big man to use humor to ease tension. A small man would have blown up. I suspect Mr. McCormack's sense of humor was one reason he was the Area Superintendent.

Congruent Words and Actions

I've discovered that natural, spontaneous humor is more than easing tension with quips, jokes or puns. A lighthearted approach to life also incorporates a talent for avoiding conflict through non-verbal communication. The expression of humorous intent using facial expressions, gestures and other body language can be learned. But, voice and body language must match. Several years ago my friend, Joe Hasenstaub, of Performance Learning Systems in California, taught me the Law of Congruence. "To communicate humor non-verbally you must be congruent," Joe explained. "You must ensure that your words and your body language match. If humor is to work, your mannerisms, facial expressions, tone of voice and other non-verbal signals must be consistent with your good intentions."

To illustrate, Joe did an experiment with me and the other instructor trainees of *Project T.E.A.C.H.*—his *Teacher Effectiveness and Classroom Handling* course for professional educators. While talking to us about the power of humor to reduce conflict in the classroom, Joe folded his arms, leaned forward and, without smiling, continued to talk. From time to time he looked off into the distance, or stared coldly at a trainee. Before long we all felt uncomfortable. We fidgeted, frowned, leaned back in our chairs and toyed with the materials on our tables. Many of us turned our faces away from him. We were uncomfortable. Joe had made his point.

When I'm happy I smile; when I'm seriously interested in someone I look at them. When I'm trusting and open I don't fold my arms. To be perceived as friendly I must act friendly. My attempts at humor must be coupled with a warm, friendly posture. Otherwise I run the risk of appearing insincere and seeming untrustworthy. Congruent words and actions convey warmth and lightheartedness.

I've also learned that to make humor work for me, I must focus on that one aspect of a situation that lends itself to a humorous response. Even in highly charged situations, humor will work for me if I'm in the right frame of mind; if I see that even what is serious can have a lighter side.

The Essence Of Humor

Seeing the cup half full instead of half empty has made my life rich. My spiritual wealth continues to grow, and I find life's lighter moments on a daily basis. One Saturday morning in particular, I remember Rotraud and I being awakened by our then three-year-old daughter, Deidre. A pair at a time she raised our eyelids as we lay asleep in our bed. "Are you in there?" she asked as she woke us up. I'm still not sure if I was or not.

Another time, our son, Jason woke us up somewhat differently. At the time he was being toilet trained. Now, I've always felt that the beginning of wisdom is to call things by their correct names. So, I always avoided using baby words with either of our children. As we arrived in his room, Jason announced somewhat stressfully, "I have to pee!"

Having the disdain that I had at the time for infantile words, and being more teacher than parent on that occasion, instead of rushing him to the toilet I tried to teach him a more acceptable expression. "Don't say 'pee', Jason," I explained, "Say 'urinate—urinate.'"

He must have thought I'd forgotten his name and what he needed to do, for he replied disconcertingly, "I no 'Eight' Daddy. I 'Jason.' I have to pee!"

My side aching with laughter, I took him . . . to "pee"!

My life is fun, and laughter is an essential part of it. But, my greatest joy lies, "not in laughter but in still smiles, which lie far deeper."

THE ESSENCE OF HUMOR IS LOVE.

Thoughts on Health & Humor

"The most completely lost of all days
is that on which one has not laughed."
- Chamfort

"He had had much experience of physicians,
and said, 'The only way to keep your health
is to eat what you don't want,
drink what you don't like,
and do what you'd druther not.'"
- Mark Twain

"Health and cheerfulness
mutually beget each other."
- Addison

Your Thoughts on Health & Humor

Deva Beck, R.N.
629 S. Rancho Santa Fe Road
Suite 354
San Marcos, CA 92069
(619) 744-1097

Deva Beck, R.N.

As a best-selling author, international speaker, and registered nurse, Deva Beck enthusiastically shares that there is a scientific relationship between the happiness of the mind and the health of the body—and that we can and do stimulate and interact with our own inherent healing processes to significantly influence the quality of our lives.

Deva's professional nursing career spans diverse areas of expertise—including health education, management, intensive care, emergency, hospice, rehabilitation, holistic health, and brain/mind research. She is uniquely qualified to bridge the gap between traditional and alternative healing approaches.

From this wide-ranging background, Deva has developed international workshops, seminars and lectures about wellness, stress management and Endorphins—for her professional peers—as well as for the fields of business, education and for people from all walks of life.

Since the discovery of the biochemical mind/body link of Endorphins, Deva has co-authored, with her husband James, The Pleasure Connection: How Endorphins Affect Our Health and Happiness, *the first easy-to-read book on this vital topic. Deva brings a fundamental synthesis to the science and art of healing—translating medical research discoveries into inspiring and informative presentations and ideas that everyone can understand and use.*

Endorphins, Humor and Health

By Deva Beck, R.N.

"How good is man's life, the mere living! How fit to employ
All the heart and the soul and the senses forever in joy!"
- Robert Browning

When I was a child, I loved to hear how laughter once helped my Dad to recover from a prolonged dizzy spell. Little did I know that I would grow up to become an expert on the biochemical rationale for his miracle cure.

Dad tells that he had been uncomfortably dizzy for more than a week—he couldn't be the active pre-teenager he'd been used to being. Forced to sit quietly most of the time, Dad was sick of being sick and fully expected to miss the next day's family outing to the beach. He just didn't feel up to it. So, he sat on the front porch, talking to a friend who'd come by. Pretty soon, they got to laughing and carrying on—as only rambunctious, unrestrained children can do—because they were relishing the memory of all the funny times they'd had together.

They laughed for more than an hour, Dad recalls. Then to his surprise—when he got up from his chair on the porch—his dizziness had disappeared. He felt well for the first time in several weeks and even went to the beach the next day. His symptoms never recurred.

More Than Runners' High

Today, more than five decades later, Endorphins have been discovered to be a medical research link between laughter and health. You've probably heard of Endorphins by now. They're your own natural biochemicals of pain-relief, happiness, and generally feeling positive, upbeat, and good about life. "Runner's high" has made Endorphins famous. But you don't have to run to get them. You have them "cooking" in your body whenever you feel euphoric. When you are most joyful, Endorphins are flowing. When you feel a chill of gladness down your spine, Endorphins are there. In fact, even as you read these words,

Endorphins are circulating throughout your body.

Endorphins are an ideal topic for an anthology like this because they're actually more than just biochemicals that flow to support a sense of happiness and a positive outlook on life. Medical science has linked the discovery of Endorphins with the body's capability to maintain health—namely our immune strength against disease. In fact, one famous Endorphin, called Beta Endorphin, is one of the front-line messengers your pituitary gland sends to your body in response to stress or other potentially harmful stimuli. Endorphins carry a communication throughout your body to be strong in its defenses and stay healthy. That's why this book about the essential connections between health, humor, and a positive approach to life would be incomplete without a chapter about Endorphins.

Exploring Endorphin Connections

There are thousands of learned articles written about Endorphins—they are an important part of the very complicated subject of brain biochemistry. But, for this chapter, you need to know just a few points about Endorphins—to help you understand the humor/health Endorphin connection.

Endorphins create euphoria and pain-relief by acting as biochemical messengers of stimuli from the outside world. They relay data from our five senses by sending and storing biochemical information within our brains and throughout our bodies.

In addition to sensory stimuli, Endorphins are involved in our emotional responses. They are found—in high concentration—in the part of our brains where emotions are experienced. Indeed, Endorphins are also biochemical messengers of emotion and mood. And—through their inherent capability to create euphoria and relieve pain—Endorphins color the way we perceive life. Through this same sense of pleasure, Endorphins are involved in our motivations to prefer certain attitudes and beliefs.

Because of this connection to our motivations, Endorphins influence the choices we make every day. In turn, these choices influence our biochemical responses, affecting future choices and events, and our ongoing interaction with life. When we choose the stimulus of laughter and a corresponding humorous attitude toward life, the biochemical flow of Endorphins—induced by laughter—supports our health and even helps us to heal when we've been ill.

Making The Choice For Laughter

An extraordinary example of this choice for a humorous attitude comes from the life of a good friend named Bea—who has been blind since early childhood. Bea has used humor all her life to help her cope with her difficulties. So it didn't surprise me that she would use humor to help her over the biggest hurdle of her life.

Over the years of stepping out confidently despite her blindness, Bea had taken many falls. So—at the age of 77—she could no longer walk, due to ongoing chronic injuries to her back. Her handicaps seemed stacked against her. Indeed—if you were to follow the prevailing medical opinion based on statistics about blind 77-year-olds—you would have predicted, as did many, that Bea would never walk again.

But her back surgeon knew he had a shot at repairing the spinal cord damage and Bea believed him. She decided to have the risky surgery and made the conscious choice to use humor—as she had always done before—to give herself better odds in her own long shot at recovery.

Returning to her home after surgery, Bea expected a light, humorous attitude from the nurses and aids who helped take care of her. (Those who took the situation or themselves too seriously usually found other jobs.) She encouraged singing and joking as part of the regular routine. She'd play games with words, purposely mispronouncing them for the fun of what they'd sound like. Puns were always the rule of the day or night and were encouraged whenever possible. Many of her helpers were assigned cute nicknames to encourage the camaraderie of fun. And—although it was weeks before Bea began to walk again—the seemingly serious and arduous task of recovery was never really noticed for the prevailing lighthearted atmosphere.

The antics of Bea's dogs and the neighboring pets were always noticed and turned into stories for visitors and telephone conversations. Asta, the guide-dog labrador, was always hungry and got into many adventures on her look-out for an interesting scrap. Loyal was the scamp of a labrador mix who delighted in escaping Bea's yard to race across the fields in the surrounding countryside. After her run, Loyal would always come to her master's chair and seem to laugh up into Bea's face, begging for a scratch behind the ears and the retrieval of some twig or branch from her silky coat. Fawn was the shy shepherd mix who would tiptoe soundlessly around the house to surprise Bea with a cold nose at unexpected times. Santos, the neighboring border collie, came over for frequent visits. Santos liked to bark and carry on in an almost conversational way. So Bea would talk to him—pretending to discuss the news of the neighborhood and gossip about other four-legged tail waggers.

Bea's pets were just typical dogs with ordinary behaviors. But their daily play was part of the good news Bea liked to hear and tell about. Their occasional outrageous gaffes made the dogs myths in their own time. Their stories were told and relished over and over.

Being an expert at reading braille, Bea made sure that she always had a jokebook or magazine with a humor section stashed beside her armchair. Occasionally, she would even read her visitors and caregivers jokes about blind people. These stories were presented under the heading of ABAPITA, "Ain't blindness a pain in the anatomy?" She instinctively knew that if she could make light of her problems with a joke or humorous story, others would be at ease with her and would enjoy life when they were in her company.

Of course, you know the outcome. Bea did learn to walk again, first progressing a few steps from her wheelchair to bed, then building on her strength with the use of a walker. After about seven months, her muscles were strong enough for Bea to put the walker aside and walk around her home without assistance. She has help from friends and family who walk with her on errands and outings to help her "see" where she is going. So now—at the age of 85—Bea has wholeheartedly proved the negative perspective wrong.

Bea's life is full of the good things she appreciates. To be sure, plenty of friends visit often and take Bea places. Its fun to be with her! There is always a new story to have a good laugh over. Or, the topic of "remember when we enjoyed..." is often a good way to pick up a sagging conversation. Bea's memory persists in focusing upon the good times. Bea "sees" life with an optimistic perspective and uses humor on a daily basis to keep it that way. She's learned to keep her Endorphins flowing.

Potent Pain-Relievers

Returning to the Endorphin details, you need to know why they are potent pain-relievers. Endorphins work in our bodies much like the pain-relieving narcotics commonly known as heroin, demerol and morphine. In fact, we now know that these related drugs work in our bodies because they are external chemical copies of our Endorphins. Endorphins are literally our own internal morphine.

Everything morphine does—Endorphins also do. They both send the same kind of message throughout our bodies—providing wonderful pain-relief and producing powerful states of euphoria. That's the good news. But the bad news is that, like morphine, Endorphins are addictive—very addictive.

I can almost hear you wondering why I'd tell you bad news about Endorphins in a book like this. You remember that I said earlier that Endorphins are triggered by stimuli coming through our five senses into our bodies. That's why we can get addicted to certain kinds of stimuli that make us feel good—even though those stimuli may be bad for us. For instance, abuse is a stimulus. So are negative behaviors and negative thinking. People can get addicted to or "locked into" negative tapes about themselves and life in general because they've learned that, in a very strange unconscious way, it feels good to feel bad. Worry and fear can be addictive mental and emotional processes that seem to require higher and higher doses of the Endorphins they've triggered. Just like a morphine addict, a worry addict may have to worry more to get a baseline dose of Endorphins from the worry stimulus. You can see how this can be a problem.

Getting Hooked On Laughter Instead Of Stress

Stress is similar. It is a proven Endorphin trigger. When Endorphins flow in response to stress, our bodies adapt through this biochemical mechanism. The famous medical researcher, Dr. Hans Selye, noted that we can cope with stress when we can adapt to it. Endorphins are involved in this adaptation process.

But stress, like worry, can be addictive. Workaholism is a well-known concept today because people have learned that the stress of heavy work loads makes them feel good—and when they get "hooked" on work—an increased burden of work makes them feel better.

But, as you've probably already guessed, you have a choice about the stimuli you can use to make you feel good. Laughter is a better choice of stimuli to trigger Endorphins. Norman Cousins made the choice of laughter famous in his book *The Anatomy of An Illness*, which recently became a television movie. The story begins when Norman became ill from a rare connective-tissue disease which was extremely painful and pronounced terminal.

Being a thoughtful and well-read man, Norman considered the situation. He knew that he had been stressed to the point of great distress in recent months. He thought he had adapted and was coping well with the stress of his work. But now he felt his own sense of powerlessness to change the problem and his profound discouragement as a result. He knew his disease was connected to this overstress response. As described in the journal *Science,* researchers at Harvard Medical School have shown that rats who undergo similar stressors—over which they have no control—do show signs of biochemical changes that indicate vulnerability to disease.

Norman knew he was discouraged and had perceived his situation to be beyond his own help to change it. Where once he'd felt capable, adaptable and powerful in response to stress—he'd enjoyed the euphoric feeling that stress can trigger—he now felt a literal stress overdose—extreme distress. His belief about himself had changed from positive to overwhelmingly negative and this was the precursor to his disease. But, he asked himself, if these negative beliefs contributed to his disease, wouldn't a change of perception about this condition and a positive belief in his own will to live, help to change his own disease process into health again?

His now famous decision to use laughter in his recovery is worth retelling in this chapter because there is strong evidence that Norman was able to trigger his own Endorphins by choosing laughter as therapy. He read joke books, watched Candid Camera clips, and countless comedies on movie film. In a conscious change of perception, Mr. Cousins encouraged himself to laugh with great energy at all the gags within these films, even the silliest and most stupid. And, he didn't settle for smiling or snickering at the comic situations. He chose to allow himself to laugh so heavily that his entire body laughed with him. (He laughed with unrestrained energy, just as my Dad had done.)

To his surprise and delight, Norman found that there was an actual anesthetic effect from ten minutes of deep laughter. This therapeutic effect then lasted two hours—allowing him pain-free sleep. When the pain returned, he then played his comedies, often to be relieved from pain once again.

Indeed, this pain-free sleep had not been achieved previously, even by high and frequent doses of demerol, the strong narcotic opiate his doctor had prescribed for pain. Pain relief equal to or better than demerol? With this important clue, we can hypothesize with confidence that laughter actually released the natural, pain-relieving Endorphin biochemistry which demerol mimics.

Through the comic perspective that laughter provided, Norman Cousins began to increase his positive belief about his own life—applying his renewed faith to the physical demands of health. And of course, he did become free of the constraint of his disease and still lives a healthy, productive life.

Making Laughter A Therapeutic Tool

Over the years of my own hospital nursing career, I have seen many examples of how a comic sense can work to influence the flow of healing. The most persuasive instance in my own personal experience came at a most unlikely time—one grey, darkening afternoon. I was on duty with a nursing colleague, named Arlene. We had worked together for several years. So I knew that, on this particular day, Arlene was as bored with the routine of hospital work as I was. I also knew that she was always "game" to have some fun despite the often depressing setting we were in.

"Hey Arlene," I said, "Let's skip vital signs!" Her eyes grew wide at my suggestion. Both of us knew, all too well, how important it was for us to take each patient's blood pressure, pulse, temperature and respirations at regular intervals. This was a ward where patients were only just recovering from heart ailments. But secretly, all of us wished for ways to break the monotonous routine of these seemingly endless procedures. "Skip vital signs?" Arlene couldn't believe her ears.

I went on, "I mean—let's skip through vital signs instead of walk, it'll be a welcome change for us and the patients." Arlene's eyes lit up. Grabbing the clipboard, she was ready for action. For a second, however, I hesitated. What about the serious hospital decorum that always seems to infect the nursing and medical staff? After all, hospitals are serious places. People are sick and dying here.

But I had already observed that the recovery of health was often accompanied by a change in attitude toward hope. When people are able to keep or regain a positive attitude—despite their physical conditions—they seem to get well quicker. I had already read about Norman Cousins and his conscious choice to use laughter as a therapeutic tool. Yes, if a serious physician or nursing supervisor discovered us skipping on the way from room to room, I had cases to cite in support for our choice to bring some fun to our evening rounds.

Looking back, I'm not sure which was more fun, the actual lighthearted action of skipping or the looks of astonished delight on the faces of our patients and their visitors. In almost every room, we surprised them with a burst of unexpected energy. Sometimes they would laugh out loud right away. Other times, we would skip lightly into a room, where we would be awakening someone who had needed an afternoon nap and was still sleeping. Then perhaps, we would see a simple smile in response to our antics.

Wherever we could, we explained that we were choosing to lighten the burden of the hospital environment, to lift people's spirits (as well as our own) and to prepare everyone's digestion for the upcoming dinner trays.

As each experience and explanation passed around the circle of rooms, we watched the ward's mood change from somber boredom to upbeat happiness and hilarity. The responses were different because the patients had their own capacity and degree of recovery. From some—we heard uproarious laughter—from others—giggles emerged. We were touched by welcome smiles that transformed faces lined with pain and suffering.

As usual, back at the central desk, the monitor-watcher carefully kept her eyes on the heartbeat tracings coming from the screens for each patient's room. Despite our unusual approach to this round of vital signs, everyone's heart kept ticking in fine order. During that hour, there were no signs of ominous EKG changes that signal danger.

As we finished in the last room, Arlene and I knew that we had an uproarious success with our experiment. We could hear laughter continuing in some of the rooms. We could feel the change in attitude—it was that palpable in the ward. We knew we had made a therapeutic difference for everybody except one.

In the room facing the nursing station, Ruby (I've changed her name for the sake of confidentiality) sat still—staring into space. In addition to a chronic heart condition, Ruby was afflicted with a catatonic state. Her face was immobilized by an uncanny mask-like expression. Ruby had not even blinked an eye for our skipping entrance. Indeed she never waivered from her frozen facial expression in the months she had been with us.

In a flash, yet another seemingly incredible idea occurred to me and I decided to act on it. "Arlene, can you still do cartwheels?" Arlene had been a college cheerleader only a few years before. "I dare you to turn a cartwheel in front of Ruby's glass door!"

By this time, Arlene was prepared for any suggestion to continue the fun. So, as I watched from the central nursing desk, Arlene removed the stethoscope from around her shoulders, pushed up her uniform sleeves and moved to the side of the ward. Quickly gathering momentum, she lightly tipped into a turn and maneuvered a perfect cartwheel right in front of Ruby's room.

Time stood still for me as I watched that instant transform an upright registered nurse into that energetic girl who had once cheered her team on to great plays. But, as fast as it had started, Arlene's transformation was over. She righted herself, sauntered back to the desk, replaced her stethoscope around her shoulders, and returned to her "proper" role.

But time must have shifted ever so slightly for Ruby. Suddenly, Arlene's nursing shoes had catapulted across Ruby's line of vision. In the briefest of momentous seconds, Ruby actually raised her eyebrows, blinked, and moved her head and face muscles in an obvious double-take at the unbelievable, outrageous event in front of her. Just for a moment, Arlene had helped Ruby escape from the prison of her catatonia and react in wonder at a fresh experience.

Even as Arlene's feet had righted themselves, Ruby's face was back to "normal." And in the months that followed, none of us ever observed another change in Ruby's mask-like face. In one second of willingness to be humorous, spontaneous and creative, a therapeutic nurse had accomplished the impossible. It was a lesson about life that I'll never forget.

In that hour, no one came to witness our therapeutic experiment with laughter and fun. Most evenings at dinner time, doctors check on their patients and supervisors drop by. I recall being relieved that we weren't "caught in the act" and reprimanded for our obvious lack of hospital decorum. But now I'm not so sure.

We knew we had made a difference in the lives of people on that ward. Indeed, in that hour, we had changed our own perspective about the value of comic relief from pain. We had gone beyond reading about the value of humor in books—we had experienced it first-hand! But we couldn't prove it by a scientific method. No follow-up studies were made, no ongoing observations confirmed the results of our experiment with humor. We didn't run Endorphin tests. But our observations confirmed that something tangible—most probably biochemical—had happened to influence attitude and health.

Laughter Gives Us Another Option

Ilana, another of my nursing colleagues, agrees that we need to reframe our attitude about responding negatively to disease. Ilana has also expanded her role as a nursing care-giver to teach workshops and seminars on living creatively through the crisis of severe illness.

Ilana opens her classes with her own story. She was born in Israel, where she worked as a nurse for many years before coming to work and teach in the United States. Ilana was assigned to an intensive-care unit in Jerusalem. Many of her patients were wounded from nearby wars—many were at "death's door" when they were brought to the hospital.

Having my own intensive-care work experience to remember, I wondered how Ilana had coped with the emotional intensity of caring for her own young countrymen who were wounded and dying from the ongoing strife in Israel? At this most depressing part of the story, Ilana added a most meaningful twist. Amid all that conflict and sadness, the nurses and doctors maintained an uproarious sense of laughter and good times. They joked almost continuously throughout their shifts. Ilana insisted that despite—and perhaps even because of—the despair all around them, the prevailing party-like atmosphere was literally fun, upbeat, and inspiring.

I wondered, how did the patients themselves react to this hilarious, seemingly incongruous situation? Then Ilana emphasized the central theme of her workshop with a typical quote from the patients—which I will paraphrase. The patients often recalled their time in intensive-care by saying, "When I arrived at the hospital, my injuries seemed so severe that I was sure I was dying. But here, amongst all of this gaiety and constant laughter, I thought, 'I must have been mistaken.' If everyone is so happy and carefree, well, I must be okay. So—with that new perception about my condition—*I found another option and I recovered.*"

Laughter brings us a new perspective—and with that fresh perception—new stimuli can come into our five senses and open new biochemical channels for Endorphins to be triggered. Laughter reduces pain, finds a way out of depression and withdrawal. Laughter can break through the addictive worry-stress-worry treadmill that leads toward overstress, a sense of hopelessness, and the inevitable ill health that follows. Laughter helps us to lay aside—if even for a moment—our outworn, too comfortable patterns of adaptation, compulsion and even addiction—to break through our rigid, limiting approaches to life. Through the stimulus of Endorphins, laughter can be the positive addiction that supports health, reinforces inherent healing mechanisms, and the fulfillment of well-being.

Don't forget that five-sensory stimuli of all kinds are involved in the triggering of Endorphins. And, because of the addictive power of Endorphin biochemistry, any of us can get addicted to the stimulus we choose. It is important, therefore, to choose wisely.

Give yourself good things, everything in moderation. Change your stimuli from time to time. Variety *is* the spice of life. Enjoy your work, enjoy your play. But if you find yourself having to work or play harder and harder to feel good, give yourself a good laugh instead. Stress leads—through potential addiction—to overstress, distress and "dis-ease."

Laughter supports a positive, flexible, hopeful attitude toward life. I know I'd much rather be addicted to laughter—wouldn't you?"

Thoughts on Health & Humor

"Make two grins grow
where there was only a grouch before."
- Elbert Hubbard

"Walking is the best possible exercise.
Habituate yourself to walk very far.
The Europeans value themselves on having
subdued the horse to the uses of man;
but I doubt whether we have not lost more
than we have gained, by the use of this animal."
- Thomas Jefferson

"A good laugh is sunshine in a house."
- Thackeray

Your Thoughts on Health & Humor

Jeffrey D. Sanderson
P.O. Box 20603
Columbus, OH 43220
(614) 771-1869

Jeffrey D. Sanderson

Jeffrey D. Sanderson was raised in a small town in northwestern Ohio. Having been ill a great deal as a child, he learned respect for what good health can mean to an individual. This encouraged him to spend most of his life studying matters of health and helping others work toward better health for themselves.

During the past thirteen years his research has included studying books, interviewing medical professionals, and investigating scientific studies. His experience in the food service industry and the computer industry helped him become aware of the proper techniques for doing his research. As a college instructor and consultant, he developed techniques for delivering his message to his audience that is both instructional and interesting. As a teacher of Senior High and Adult Bible classes, as well as a student of the Bible, he learned the true meaning of good health and how to make it more meaningful for others. As he collected his data, he correlated facts, discarded hearsay and compiled knowledgeable data and opinions.

Jeffrey has developed a unique approach to the meaning of good health as well as what one must do to achieve and maintain it. His outlook encompasses the whole of one's life, not just one aspect of it, and it is directed toward the average person who wants to live a productive, healthy life.

Good Health is More Than Exercise

By Jeffrey D. Sanderson

"Better to hunt in fields, for health unbought,
Than fee the doctor for a nauseous draught.
The wise, for cure, on exercise depend;
God never made his work, for man to mend."
- John Dryden

I've been studying health for a number of years now, and the health craze that is going on has me somewhat alarmed. It seems that there has been a proliferation of the idea that if you exercise regularly you will be assured of maintaining good health. While exercise itself is an important part of a good health maintenance program, it is by far not the only thing to take into consideration. There are many factors involved in achieving good health and maintaining it throughout your life. Ignore any of these, and some aspect of your health will suffer as a result.

The human body is a complex mechanism, and as such it relies on many things for a particular need. As an example, let's look at the muscles in the body. Most people would think that in order to maintain good muscle tone that they must exercise. This is true. However, this is not the whole truth. In order to maintain good muscle tone, you must exercise regularly AND eat the right kinds of proteins to maintain the muscle AND eat the right kind of carbohydrates to prevent loss of muscle AND rest the muscle properly in order to allow it to heal. Neglect any part of this and you defeat your purpose as well as run the risk of turning your muscle into worthless sludge.

In order to make sure that this doesn't happen, I stress the importance of a comprehensive health program—a program that looks at all aspects of the body rather than just one or two. For the sake of sanity, I have categorized the various needs for good health into five easy to identify areas—time management, diet, hygiene, exercise, and rest. In order to achieve and maintain good health, you should implement a program that encompasses all five categories.

Time Management

Typically, when I talk with people about implementing a total health program for themselves, their first reaction to time management is one of surprise. Most people don't even think about it as being a part of maintaining good health, let alone working it into their overall health program. After all, isn't time management something that executives use to be three places at once? What does that have to do with health?

There are two reasons for including proper time management into a comprehensive health program. To illustrate the first reason, let me ask this—how many times have you said something like, "I'd like to exercise more often, but I just don't have time"...or, "I'd like to get more rest during the day, but I just don't have time"...or, "I'd like to eat better, but I just don't have time"?

By learning to properly manage your time, you can be sure to do the things that will provide you with better health. You will schedule those things that are most important to you on a daily basis. This means that all of those things that you currently neglect because of time (such as eating properly and exercising) will now be on your schedule. You will be assured of getting them done!

The second reason for time management is to relieve stress. The time management program that I teach compels you to set priorities for your life. You make commitments to those that are most important to you, you examine what you really want out of life, and you prioritize your time and your activities accordingly. By doing this you relieve up front a lot of the stress that most people go through on a daily basis. Small decisions about what to do and when are already resolved before the decision needs to be made. When a spot decision is necessary, your priorities make that decision a lot easier. And because you make your decisions intelligently based upon the priorities that YOU have previously set for your life, you don't spend time worrying about whether or not you made the proper decision. You already know.

Diet

A proper diet is something that you have had pushed at you since you were a child. Your mother always tried to force food down you that you didn't like, just because (she said) the food was good for you. Now that you're grown up, you understand why...or do you? It is estimated that well over 60% of the population of the United States is overweight. This overweight state is not only due to overeating, but to eating the wrong types of foods. Many people are still rebelling against their parents by not eating the foods that are good for them. They feel they are in control that way. Others simply are not going to eat what they don't like and they aren't going to try to find out what foods they like and what foods they don't, because they would rather stay with the same fattening foods they've been eating all along. Try getting someone who eats biscuits and gravy for breakfast to eat broccoli for lunch! It's not a pretty sight.

Whatever your reason for eating wrong, understand this—you cannot maintain good health while you are eating incorrectly. Why? Think of it this way. Your body is a conglomeration of cells. The nutrients in what you eat become the fuel for all the cells in the body. This fuel is used by the cell to keep it functioning properly. Each group of similar cells (e.g., muscle, brain) requires different nutrients to survive. A diet out of balance will favor one group, but harm another group. For this reason, it is extremely important that you eat a balanced diet, that is, a diet that contains food from the four basic food groups of Meat, Fish and Poultry; Dairy Products; Fruits and Vegetables; and Breads, Cereals and Grains. Eating a balanced diet will insure that the various nutritional needs of the body will be met.

As important as it is to eat a balanced diet, it is equally important to eat the proper amount. There are two possible ways to not eat properly. You either eat too much, or you don't eat enough. Keep in mind here that when I talk about how much you eat, I'm talking about your NUTRITIONAL intake, not the quantity of food itself. You can eat large quantities of food, and not get much nutrition, just as you can eat small quantities of food and get a lot of nutrition. A good structure for you to follow in order to determine how well you are eating is the United States Recommended Daily Allowance (USRDA) charts. While these charts are based on averages, and as such are far from perfect, they are the only real reference that we have at the current time. In addition to this, most foods purchased have their nutritional information according to the USRDA printed on the label. This makes it easy to monitor your intake. I have found that if you keep your nutritional intake between 100% and 200% of the USRDA, then you are maintaining the proper amount.

The foods that you eat depend upon your tastes. Good foods don't have to, and typically don't, taste bad. Find some good recipes and experiment a little. You don't have to get weird. Just stick to the basics and make them pleasant tasting. You'll be surprised at how good some foods taste that you have not eaten before. In general, remember the following rules:

First, keep the fat content in your diet low. When fats or oils must be used, use vegetable products rather than animal fats. Drink low-fat milk. Keep ice cream and similar products to a minimum.

Second, keep the fiber content in your diet high. This can be accomplished by eating lots of fresh vegetables, fruits and grains.

Third, eat more freshwater fish and skinless poultry. Reduce the amount of red meat that you eat and eat the leanest cuts. The leaner cuts cost more, but you will benefit from it in the long run.

I would also recommend that, as much as possible, you fix your own meals rather than eating in restaurants. This way you are assured of knowing exactly what is in the food you are eating, and how it has been prepared.

Hygiene

Why hygiene? Well, according to the research that I have done, it is clear that good personal hygiene is one of the main reasons why the United States is so far ahead of other countries when it comes to eliminating infectious diseases and illnesses. Daily bathing and general cleanliness keep away the bacteria that cause them. In general, you should bathe daily, wash your hands regularly throughout the day and brush your teeth and gums after eating and before bedtime. This will not only keep you healthier, but will help keep your family and close friends smiling as well!

I know that this sounds like the same old routine you've been hearing for years, and you're right. It is. But you know what? It works and it's important. So before you pass it off as the same old thing, make sure you aren't ignoring something that you shouldn't. Examine your own personal hygiene habits closely. Are there areas where you need change? If so, make the necessary change. You can only benefit from it.

Exercise

As I mentioned earlier, exercise is an important part of any comprehensive health program. But there's more to exercise than going out and killing yourself for an hour. You need to pay careful attention to what exercises you do, how you do them and the intensity with which you do them. Exercise comes in two flavors—aerobic exercise and anaerobic exercise. Both are important, but achieve different results.

Aerobic exercise is what you hear about most. This is the type of exercise that is sustained long enough that the muscles need to draw oxygen from other parts of the body in order to have enough energy to do the work. Aerobic exercise strengthens the cardiovascular system (heart, lungs, circulation).

Examples of aerobic exercise include brisk walking, aerobic dance, and running. Anything that keeps your heart rate up for an extended period of time qualifies. I recommend that you pick three days during the week to do aerobic exercise. These days should be non-consecutive days such as Monday, Wednesday and Friday, or Tuesday, Thursday and Saturday.

Anaerobic exercise is exercise that happens quickly and can generally be accomplished by using the muscle's energy reserves. Anaerobic exercise strengthens the muscle itself, and, depending on the exercise, can help you develop coordination and agility.

Examples of anaerobic exercise include weight lifting, volleyball, and racquetball. Any exercise that requires strength in short bursts qualifies. I recommend that you pick three days during the week to do anaerobic exercise. Like aerobics, these days should be non-consecutive days such as Monday, Wednesday and Friday or Tuesday, Thursday and Saturday, but should not be the same day as the day you do aerobics.

Don't forget when you exercise to stretch your muscles both before and after the exercise. Allow yourself a slow pace at first to get your body to "warm up" to the exercise, and when finished, slow down gradually to allow your body a chance to "cool down" from the exercise. Doing this will reduce your chances of injury, which will prevent you from writing to me from a hospital bed complaining about doing these exercises.

Rest

My last category in a comprehensive health program is one that too many people ignore—rest. It sounds simple enough. You sleep at night, so that's your rest. However, there is a little more to it than that. Rest is one of the more important aspects of good health, and should be treated accordingly. It comes in three different types—sleep, breaks and play.

Sleep is the most common form of rest. In order for you to get the most rest from sleep, you should go to bed early and get up early. There's an old adage that "an hour of sleep before midnight is worth two hours after." This seems to be true for most people. Just as important is learning how much sleep is required by your body. You need to adjust your sleeping habits to match what your body needs. Too much sleep can have the same effect on you as too little sleep. If you're getting the proper amount, you should wake up refreshed and ready to start the day.

Breaks are another important part of rest. No matter what you are doing, it is important for you both mentally and physically to take periodic breaks. I recommend that every twenty minutes or so you just stop what you are doing and focus your attention on something else for a minute or so. Every couple of hours you should physically walk away from what you are doing for about five or ten minutes. Following this procedure will keep you refreshed, alleviate fatigue and enable you to more closely focus your attention on what you are doing.

Another form of break that is most beneficial is the meditation break. I would recommend that at least once a day you take a 10 minute meditation break. What exactly is a meditation break? It is a period of quiet time without interruption. In order to get the full benefit of this break, find a quiet place where you are away from outside noise and where you won't be disturbed. Then, for a period of at least ten minutes, sit quietly in a chair with your hands in your lap, or on the floor with your legs crossed and your hands in your lap. Listen to your breathing and concentrate on it. Don't allow anything else to enter your mind. This technique forces you to remove yourself from all tensions and stress. Try it. You will be pleasantly surprised at how rested and relaxed you feel afterward.

As we become older we tend to forget about the importance of play in our daily activities. It is important to spend time doing things that you enjoy from both a mental and physical standpoint. Allow time during each day to play some cards or a game of checkers or something similar. Sitting around telling jokes with your friends always makes you feel better. Whatever you enjoy that will take you away from your normal daily routine. It helps keep your mind alert, and gives your body a chance to recuperate.

Change Your Focus

This has been an overview of my comprehensive health philosophies. As you consider these ideas, keep in mind that my viewpoint of good health is somewhat different from what you have been bombarded with by the media. The popular view of good health seems to focus on having a long life. I know many people who work at trying to live longer. So far, none of them have been able to answer this simple question: "Longer than what?" Longer than you would live otherwise? How do you know?

The point that I am making is that exercising for a longer life is the wrong focus. Somehow an image of good health persists that if you do all the right things, you won't die. Or at least you won't die for a very long time...which in itself is relative to the individual. Our lives are complicated these days, and there are so many things other than one's health that can determine life and death, that it doesn't make sense to focus on having a long life.

Where then should the focus be? It should be on now—the current moment. Each of us is here for a purpose. We have something to accomplish. How, then, can we achieve that purpose if we are not healthy? If we spend most of our time sick in bed, how much can we get accomplished? I believe that it is necessary, and even the responsibility of everyone, to be as healthy as he or she can be. Not for later, but for now. So that each person can accomplish what he or she is meant to accomplish TODAY, and tomorrow, and the next day.

If you do what is necessary to maintain good health, then you will always be ready to meet whatever challenges life has to offer. You will be able to work each day toward achieving your goals in life.

And, should you be one of the fortunate ones to achieve a long life, you will still be able to live each day to its fullest.

Thoughts on Health & Humor

"Exercise and temperance
can preserve something of our early strength
even in old age."
- Cicero

"Good humor may be said to be
one of the very best articles of dress
one can wear in society."
- Thackeray

"Nothing is as funny as
something done in all seriousness."
- Will Rogers

Your Thoughts on Health & Humor

Mike Duckworth
Priority #1 - The Customer
5056 Greenberry Drive
Sacramento, CA 95841
(916) 332-8668

Mike Duckworth

Powerful, Motivating, Entertaining, Down to earth, Exciting, and Value-packed are terms the audiences of Mike Duckworth use in describing his presentations .

No issue causes more concern in the business community today than that of Customer Service through SATISFACTION. The challenge and Mission of this economy during the 1990's is establishing our customer, client, patient, student and constituent as our #l Priority. No one has a clearer picture of this opportunity than this professional speaker, writer, trainer and consultant.

Mike's I CARE mission, message and mentality are contagious. He brings to his audiences the experiences of "being there, on the firing line, toe to toe, face to face with the CUSTOMER." His practical, personal perspective was shaped during the twenty-six years he spent in sales and sales management with two of the largest retailers in the world, Montgomery Ward and Sears Roebuck. His background includes positions as commissioned sales person, store manager, and district merchandiser. He has either sold or caused to be sold over 327 MILLION DOLLARS in products and services.

He is an active member of Toastmasters International, the National Speakers Association and the International Customer Service Association.

Mike Duckworth and his wife, Carol, are the parents of four daughters and grandparents of two strapping boys just beginning to walk.

The following chapter is an excerpt from his forthcoming book "How to Become Priority #1."

Humor Helps ...It Saved My Life

By Mike Duckworth

"Man is the only creature endowed with the power of laughter"

- Greville

Each time I took a breath the struggle seemed to be more than it was worth. Desperation began to set in in spite of my drugged Demoral daze. I heard the doctor tell my nurse, "His wife better be here within thirty minutes or it will be too late."

I remember thinking quite clearly, "It's time to begin taking this situation a little more seriously." I was in the Sacramento Sutter Memorial Hospital intensive care unit. It was 2:27 a.m. on a stormy morning in March 1983. I had undergone bypass surgery just two days earlier. My temperature was 104 degrees, my blood pressure was skyrocketing and my lungs had filled up with fluid. I was dying.

More than 150,000 bypass surgeries were performed in 1983. Less than three percent of these resulted in serious complications. I mumbled the phrases that had become my litany of misery in those dark months. "Life is too short to put up with this pain and aggravation. Why in the world do these things continue to happen to me? What did I do to deserve this?"

As if in answer to these whispered questions my nurse, Stephanie, entered the room in her pale green scrubs. Smiling reassuringly, looking quickly over her shoulder to be certain no one would overhear, she placed a firm, compassionate hand on my forearm, and crouched down by the side of my bed. She whispered in a soft voice, "You are messing up my entire day. If you had any idea of the paperwork involved in terminations you wouldn't be screwing around like this. My shift changes at seven a.m.and I have a breakfast date. Now you have a little over two hours to pull out of this. Let's get with it, Michael!"

Stephanie's words and dry wit yanked me back from the abyss into which I was about to plummet. She made a **positive difference** in my life through a risk with humor. I lifted my right hand circling the thumb and forefinger signifying "OK!" and panted with a grin, "You're something else." My poor me attitude began to vanish forever.

Surgeons tell me that this behavior is not common and certainly not encouraged among the highly trained, very competant nursing elite to be found in major hospital intensive care units. The environment that exists for malpractice litigation certainly must have given her pause to think. What would lead Stephanie to take such an exceptional risk?

She answered my question two days later just before I was moved to a more conventional hospital room in the cardiac care unit. "First, you demonstrated your sense of humor with that dumb cartoon; second, you showed you cared about living; and third you made me care enough to reach out to you in a special way. The doctors, nurses, drugs and equipment are only minor when compared to a patient's attitude and perspective. You allowed us to find a way to help you."

Prior to that winter morning in 1983, I spent several weeks obsessed with the idea that my days were numbered. I arrived at the hospital in the frame of mind that if I was going to check out, the last impression of me was not going to be one of just another uptight, driven, type A, corporate casualty who continued to dictate and demand until the end. Not this time. I was determined to lighten up, follow orders without passing judgement, and be a pleasure to be around. I had a compulsion to lighten the load of others. They responded, though not as dramatically as Stephanie, to lighten mine. This was the lesson I carried away from that hospital sixteen days later and have kept brightly polished since.

I tell this story in many of my presentations. From my point of view it is obviously *perfect performance* from a customer service standpoint. This started out as just one of those personal stories that help illustrate that *taking calculated risks with humor can ease some of our major crises.* Our lives continue to *evolve* and *generate* new perspectives through this type of *learning.*

Humor Happens

My wife, Carol, clipped the dumb cartoon Stephanie mentioned from "Parade Magazine" the Sunday before I entered the hospital. We brought it to the hospital with us the afternoon prior to the operation. I used it as a bookmark for *In Search of Excellence* by Tom Peters.

Inevitably doctors, nurses and hospital support personnel asked what I was reading, picked up the book, made a comment on its value and examined the cartoon. Each had a positive personal reaction to this little nugget. These professionals sought out and pounced on this little piece of newsprint as a way of personalizing their objective, *to ease my pain both physically and mentally.* It took them *out of their normal routine and allowed them to share my sense of humor.*

"For Pete's sake, let's operate! While we stand here, he's getting well all by himself!"

It is an odd feeling to look back and measure the cumulative effect of that thoughtful gift of humor.

I believe the combination of that tiny feature from "Laugh Parade" and Tom Peters' fine book on business excellence were the seeds that took root and blossomed into a speaking, training and writing business today.

We create our own circumstances for fulfillment. Carol's instinctive action with the Sunday paper and a pair of scissors helped pull me out of my gloom, and allowed me to share a smile with others. This gave *them* a special feeling of happiness.

This act also set us on the path for a new career. The myth of luck or coincidence does not apply here. Open hearts and minds make things happen. They create **synchronicity**.

Humor Hunt

I followed instructions to the letter and completed my homework. The local P.B.S. channel aired a full hour and a half color special on bypass surgery the week before. I had absolute confidence in the professional operating team at my disposal.

Shortly after I arrived at the hospital George Miller, my surgeon, dropped in to discuss my surgery the following morning, and answer any questions I had. He pointed out that this procedure was not without risk. He drew a sketch of the six bypasses he and my cardiologist Steve Morrison had planned. He indicated that veins from both my left leg and upper chest would be used to create the new plumbing. While I examined the sketch he picked up my book and inspected the clipping.

I was told that this particular cardiac surgeon was the best I could ask for. If he had a weakness, however, it was his bedside manner. The last thing I wanted to do was give him a reason to be offended. He stood above my bed, peered over his glasses and said with a chuckle, "It's been a tough day, I needed that." I returned his drawing with a sigh and answered, "I hope you're a better plumber than an artist."

This verbal exchange took less than ten seconds. That small investment in time and the search for a smile brought us to a level beyond a doctor-patient relationship. The bond we now had was more personal and lasting.

As I lay in my hospital bed I realized that I had been able to create stressful situations all my life by:

- Taking myself too seriously
- Failing to see and achieve balance
- Exhausting myself in preparation
- Establishing the wrong priorities.

The sixteen days I spent in this facility allowed me to put my life and purpose into proper perspective. A single theme seemed to run throughout the entire experence. I began a hunt for humor much like I had searched for Easter eggs during my childhood. Finally the light dawned. In my hurry I had run by or stepped on more brightly packaged treasures of fun than I had acquired. When I began to relax, listen and participate, I found that it wasn't my job to be the center of attention all the time. I could be much more effective by sharing the spotlight.

About seven-thirty that evening a young man appeared at my door and proclaimed that he was there to assist me in preparing for the surgery the following day. "How?" I asked.

"I am your barber. I am here to relieve you of all your bodily hair from the neck down," he answered with a winning smile.

Patient: I hope you packed a lunch.

Technician: I see what you mean, this is a two razor job.

Patient: You've found the missing link.

Technician: More like the missing link' s dad.

Patient: Hope you didn't have plans for this evening.

Technician: May I use your phone, she'll never believe this.

Patient: Take her the proof.

Technician: I left my pickup at home.

Patient: Do you have any idea how long it took to grow all this?

Technician: No, but drink some Ortho, it'll grow back faster than your lawn.

Patient: Are you sure this is necessary?

Technician: Don't laugh, I got a patient mixed up once. He had a hairy hide just like yours. I got as far as the mark of Zorro just like this, zip, zip, zip. Then we figured out that overnight observation did not require a shave. I'm sure he had some great stories to tell by the pool for a few weeks. I know you're getting chilly. About half of my customers start sweating as I work my way down.

Patient: I'll be as quiet as a mouse. The last thing I want to do is distract you at this point.

All it took was forty-five minutes. What could have been a tortuous assault on my dignity turned into a relatively painless procedure handled by a professional He shared the spotlight with me and left me with the pink and tender skin of a three year old and a smile on my face.

I'm certain that his was a set routine for occasions and conditions like mine. He had an attitude and a presence about him that made his task seem almost joyful.

We hunted for humor together and were delighted with the result.

Humor Hunger

The hour of the knife approached. Those around me began to show the strain. Tones of voice changed, steps quickened, the monitor was watched more carefully and breathing seemed to become louder.

I had a few moments to myself. The temptation was too great to pass up. I reached for the surgical tape lying on the table by my bed and the cartoon from the nightstand. It was time to lighten things up a little bit!

I was wheeled out of my room on a cloud of valium to the holding area referred to as the "launching pad." We were quite a group: two friends, three of my four daughters, nurse, driver and brave but embattled wife. We were a peculiar sight. Eight long faces and a giggling goon on a gurney. Carol and I were left alone to have a private conversation outside the swinging doors of the operating area. She looked like I should have felt. No words can express the uncertainty and fear in those wide, brown eyes.

I did the best I could to reassure her with the normal last minute promises and asked her to lean over for a final "I'll-see-you-later-kiss." She began to straighten up as I moved the sheet down to the bottom of my rib cage. I had plastered the newsprint firmly to my freshly shaved chest. She smiled readily through the tears and punched me lightly on the shoulder as if to say, "You fool, I love you."

Operating rooms are clinical, sterile, no-nonsense places where professionals work diligently to save or enhance life. I've seen and read enough stories to know this is all true until the patient "zonks out." Then the music goes on and the humor starts. All I wanted was a tiny piece of the action. I tasted the peculiar garlic flavor of the anesthetic, and began my count down from 100. At 97 one of the several nurses in attendence lifted the drape with one hand and was about to apply the mustard colored brush to my chest with the other. She exclaimed with delight, "Come look at this. You won't believe this guy."

The last thing I remember that morning were faces appearing above me, capped and masked in surgical green and eyes crinkled at the corners that seemed to say, "This is special—a fun one."

Someone from that team taped the worn little cartoon to the front of my chart and sent it up with me to the intensive care unit.

My crisis nearly two days later, I am assured, was about average. My impression was that I couldn't stay focused. "Your wife is on the way." Stephanie's lips were no more than six inches from my ear but her voice sounded as if it were coming from a cellar.

"Great! She'll know what to do," I gasped.

Then panic set in. Thoughts began to cascade: *The weather's terrible, she hates driving in weather like this...wind must be 30 m.p.h., rain blowing right into her windshield...I'm so thirsty I'd love a popsicle right now...are the bills paid?...it's 2:43, time is slipping away...*

George Miller's voice: "You're in trouble, Mike, we need you to help us. We can't stand around and wait much longer, you're obviously not going to get better by yourself." His hand rested gently on my unkempt, moist head to reassure me.

Human beings have the ability to share laughter, amusement and fun with each other. Occasionally we wait too long to extend or accept the invitation to this banquet of understanding. Our thirst and hunger go unquenched. In this case the response was in time.

The actions taken in the next few minutes were a study in effective use of time and effort. At the end, Dr. George announced to all that this was the "finest handling of this procedure" he had ever seen. If it had been possible, I would have given the medical team a standing ovation. Patting my right hand on the bed was all that I could manage.

Humor Hazards:

Our "funnybones" can be tickled by amusement and hilarity, but they can also be bruised or broken through crude, caustic and careless remarks.

Tough questions need to be asked. Our consistent evaluation of our effect on other people requires that we objectively search our performance for flaws that require purging.

Do I work too hard at sharing my amusement?
Do I become lazy and thoughtless in humor?
Do I take my SENSE of humor for granted?
Do I use laughter as a crutch?
Do I withhold my humor as a weapon?
Do I use hilarity as a hammer?
Do I take myself too seriously?
Do I demand the center of attention?
Do I feel more comfortable being the *joke, joker* or *jokee?*
Do I fail to listen?
Do I fail to try?

I frequently find that my attitudes and perceptions are not well formed because I fail to understand their effect on other people.

We must *weave humor into our personal fabric* to both strengthen and bond our relationships.

Recognizing warning signals in those we seek to persuade, teach, motivate and entertain is a skill we must establish if we wish to avoid these hazards.

Humor Hints:

There is evidence that ancient man expressed and understood laughter and entertainment before the use of language was developed. I'm certain that the same frustrations faced our ancestors that face us today. The walls of caves are covered with the hieroglyphic equivalents of, "You had to be there..." "Well, it was funny at the time..." and,"I just can't seem to remember a punch line."

The frustrations associated with planned humor are common to any acquired skill. Nothing replaces *practice, attention to detail and purposeful spontaneity*. Our creative ability in this area can be compared to a discussion on fencing I saw in a movie as a child. "Hold it like you would a bird," the instructor told the prince. "Just firmly enough to keep it from escaping but gently enough to keep from crushing it."

The ability to create the *fresh air of fun* in an environment through the use of our intellect and instinct sets us apart from those who wish to cloak it in a mist of dreary, repetitive routine.

Add to the list below your own ideas for habits you wish to establish in your humor development.

Do I share or give the spotlight *easily?*

Do I trust my instincts to allow my *humor sense* to be contagious?

Do I identify my *purpose* for the laughter and smiles created?

Do I establish and *perpetuate relationships* with humor?

Do I *invest* in the happiness of others?

Do I look for humor or do I let it *surprise* me?

Do I use levity to reflect *good taste?*

Do I use mirth to be the *positive exception?*

Do I *establish the standard?*

Humor Hypothesis

Philosophers, theorists and humorists have spent centuries analyzing this *most powerful of human traits, the ability to cause ourselves and others happiness.* Humor is an intensely personalized gift of intellect as different in each of us as our fingerprints and D.N.A. chemistry.

As a professional speaker and writer it is incumbent upon me to entertain with a purpose. The ability to illustrate a serious point lightly is essential.

The lessons I learned during the winter of 1983 were dramatic and in some surprising ways, miraculous.

I left the hospital hooked up to a portable oxygen tank. The rain had just stopped; the air was crisp and clear; leaves, grass and lights were never greener. I was not judged ready to be discharged yet but they had acceded to my request when I insisted that I was not spending another night away from home.

As we pulled away from the curb, I dropped my hand to the side of the bucket seat and pulled out a folded letter-size piece of paper dated January 3, 1983. It listed the six things I had to do that day;

1. Change career
2. Inventory prep
3. Work prospect file
4. Handle Jacobs complaint
5. Get orders out
6. Check sale signing

Welcome to the wonderful world of retail. I felt the same dread begin to creep in on me that I had felt so many times before. With the obvious exception of number one, none of the items listed were anything close to what I enjoyed or wanted to be doing with my working life, I tore the list in half, then in quarters and finally into pieces the size of confetti.

I resolved to walk away from an attitude of hopelessness just as I had walked from the hospital that morning. I had been given another chance. I would not fail to take full advantage of it.

The sheer wonder and joy of that morning allowed me to savor the experience of living. Life is entirely too short to allow ourselves to be held hostage by the grim faces life can put in our mirrors each morning.

I established an entirely different mind set. It was much more important for me to:

- Slow down and listen.
- Spend more time with my family.
- Look for ways to enjoy each day.
- Find ways to share my knowledge—teach.
- Open my mind to other peoples' ideas.
- Become a positive difference in others' lives.
- Laugh more often.

Every major success I have achieved has come from energy within. It has been stoked with **purpose, preparation, perspective, persistance** and **performance** with the attitude that **I CARE** (*competence, awareness, responsiveness* and *excellence*.)

The helping hand of humor plays a significant role in each of these precepts. Without it our journey turns stale and lifeless.

What if it were true
that **laughter** could be used as a catalyst to **awaken dreams, purpose, vision** and the **mission** in our lives?

What if it were true
that the **joy** of the human spirit is **released** through a **smile**?

What if it were true
that **joy** was **contagious**?

What if it were true
that those contagions we acquired were **optimism** and an **"I can" mentality**?

What if it were true
that if we allowed ourselves to be affected continuously by this **prescription** we would begin an **epidemic of laughter**?

What if it were true
that understanding our own foibles and idiosyncrasies was the **key to motivaton**?

What if it were true
that the gentle velvet touch of humor could ignite the **imagination** of an individual or group to further a **common purpose**?

What if it were true
that **levity** was a **common language** and a truly international **bonding agent**?

What if it were true
that the use of humor as a principle **communicating skill** would produce a more global **understanding of opportunity?**

What if it were true
that this **exercise** was **unlimited** and the **possibilities** were **infinite**?

What if it were true
that **humor offers hope** after all?

This work is dedicated
to the memory of
Bill Hoest,
my cartoonist friend
whom I will never
have a chance to meet.
He passed away in November of 1988.

- Michael Duckworth

Thoughts on Health & Humor

"You grow up the day you have your first real laugh — at yourself."
- Ethel Barrymore

"Those who bring sunshine to the lives of others cannot keep it from themselves."
- Sir James Barrie

"When I wake up each morning,
I always do my exercises. I tell myself sternly,
'Ready now. Up-down-up-down.'
After three strenuous minutes of this,
I then do the same thing with my other eyelid."
- Jackie Gleason

Your Thoughts on Health & Humor

Dorothy Ellis
1401 3rd Street, Suite 18
Sacramento, CA 95814
(916) 448-3368

Dorothy Ellis

Dorothy Ellis, M.A., a successful public speaker, vocalist and author, is a native Bostonian who credits her parents with instilling in her a love for learning and music. Her years of pursuing a college education while raising a family taught her that she possessed the confidence to accept a challenge and the ability to achieve goals.

Her goals constantly changed as she pursued her career in education Beginning as a parent education teacher, she became coordinator of infant and child development centers for the Hacienda La Puente Unified School District, La Puente, California.

Becoming increasingly aware of the need for special programs for families at risk of child abuse, she co-authored a grant which enabled her to create and facilitate specialized classes, and to produce videos to teach positive parenting skills. These videos became the foundation for a parent education program which is used as a model today throughout California. At California State University, Northridge, as an Assistant Professor, she taught seminars in child development.

In 1985, Dorothy accepted another challenge and moved to Sacramento to accept a position with the State Department of Social Services as a Specialist in Child Abuse Prevention. Now, several years later, she has combined her talents, years of experience, and a unique ability to communicate, into a blend which audiences find most stimulating.

Dorothy is a speaker with the ability to teach, motivate and entertain her audience. She is an active participant in Toastmasters International, and has received several awards at district and regional levels in humorous and motivational speech contests.

She received her B.A. and M.A. in Human Development from Pacific Oaks College, Pasadena, California. She has earned an adult education credential, a standard teaching credential and an administrative credential.

Dorothy has appeared on radio and television. During a recent interview, the interviewer stated that Dorothy has a zest for life that is contagious.

Dream On

By Dorothy Ellis

Go confidently in the direction of your dreams!
Live the life you've imagined!
- Henry David Thoreau

Music of the Heart

A myriad of color, a rainbow in motion floated across the room. It was a barefoot little girl, dressed in silks of many colors. The child's long, dark curls swirled about her face as she twirled and pirouetted across her stage. The music faded. She smiled, curtsied and blew kisses to the audience she was dreaming of. Then she ran behind her curtain. She was so proud.

The little girl had created her own dance and she had designed her costume all by herself. The costume was the result of her rummaging through her mother's bureau drawers, finding just what she wanted, then wrapping herself in her mother's colorful scarves and belts. Oh yes, she had even named her performance. She called it, "My Rainbow Scarf Dance."

On With the Show

He stood in front of the open garage. He wore a T-shirt, worn jeans and a sequined, glittery hat that said, "Happy New Year." Removing the hat with a sweeping motion, he bowed low to his audience, then stood erect, reached into his pockets, removed his hidden treasures and began.

As he juggled brightly colored balls, his watchful audience—composed of every kid in the neighborhood he could cajole, wheedle or bribe to come to his juggling and magic show—came to life, yelling, "More, more, more!"

Into the Wild Blue Yonder

It was mid-morning. The sun felt warm on his face as the boy stared out the classroom window mesmerized by the pattern made from the leaves blowing in the spring breeze. He was a daring pilot known for his daring feats in the sky. But, his air show was ended abruptly by a voice breaking his reverie. "Are you daydreaming again?

Later that day, at the dinner table, this child excitedly began to tell his father what he had seen as he walked home from school. His eyes grew wide as he breathlessly described his adventure. Interrupting his dinner just long enough to glance over at his son, the father asked, "Are you making up one of your crazy stories again?" The message was clear. Silently, the boy finished his dinner.

Crushed Dreams

With brush in hand and watercolors spread before her, the child began to paint. She dreamed she was a great artist painting a piece for a famous museum. It was beginning to take shape. She completed the last few strokes on the trunk and branches, then started to create, with her brush, the green leaves.

She sensed someone looking over her shoulder. "Does that look like a tree to you?" She looked down. Her shoulders slumped. She was crushed. She would never be a famous artist. Why, she couldn't even paint a tree that looked like a tree.

Joy and Defeat

Four stories about four children. Each laughed. Each played. Each dreamed. But here the similarity ends. The first two children experienced joy and fulfillment in acting out their dreams. The other two children saw their dreams shattered.

Do incidents like these affect a child's life? I say they do. And I know, because I was that little girl painting the tree. And the little girl who danced? Today she designs beautiful costumes and choreographs dances on a real stage. The dreams of her childhood became the realities of her adulthood.

Dreams of the Young

Have you ever observed how a young child becomes completely absorbed in the moment and is often oblivious to all else? Dr. Burton White, researcher at the Harvard University Pre-School Project, notes that children who spend as much as 20 per cent of their time with their attention focused on an object, or who appear to be staring or daydreaming, are the happiest and brightest children. "This," he said, "seems to be a small child's way to seek out an identity and to grasp knowledge of the great big world that is out there."

A dear friend of mine, who is visually handicapped, shared with me that his earliest childhood memories always were centered around music. He saw himself as a famous orchestra conductor—one who had skillfully mastered many instruments. During his childhood, he was often accused of daydreaming and of not paying attention. School years were difficult years for him. "But," he said, "the one thing that anchored me during these stormy years was the vision—the dream—of being a famous musician."

Just his childhood dream? Hardly. Today he is an accomplished pianist who has seen his dream become his reality.

Another friend guided me through his newly acquired art studio. His pride was obvious. Here is where he would begin to sculpt. The pile of wood stacked against one wall would soon become frames for stretching canvases. Paints, bags of clay, pastels—all were stacked neatly on shelves awaiting the artist's touch to turn them into original works of art.

I noticed a half-finished silhouette on an easel and another on a wall. My friend laughed as he told me, that when he was about seven, he loved to make what he called "shadow people" with his fingers. Now, the "shadow people" of his childhood are becoming his beautiful silhouettes.

"All I wanted to do, when I was a kid, was to draw," he told me. "But nobody encouraged me. In fact they did everything they could to discourage me."

So he did what his parents expected of him. He got a nine-to-five job. But when he was in his late thirties, the realization that he had never followed his dream came to him. He had had just one dream—to draw, to paint, to create. And now, five years after leaving the job he disliked to study art, he was ready to commit his life to his dream. The hands of his youth, that made shadows on walls, are now creating beauty many people can enjoy.

Lost Dreams

As children, our daydreams are limitless. It is when we grow out of those early childhood years that we begin to label our dreams and pass judgement on them. We're told that life is serious. And then we're told it's time to forget those silly dreams and get down to the business of life.

And so we get down to the serious business of life which may result in our giving up who we truly want to be and in our ignoring the voice of our child within—the child who holds our dreams and our visions. Thus, we go through life never really becoming the person we want to become.

If you are one who has lost sight of your childhood dreams, perhaps these words of mine will awaken the child that sleeps within you:

Do you know how to laugh?
Do you know how to sing?
Do you know the joy a tender word can bring?
Do you tingle with excitement when you
hear the ocean roar?
That's your child within.

You may be only five years old
Or you may be fifty nine
Your face may have the bloom of youth
Or it may be softly lined
Shiny curls of childhood or hair of silver gray
We all have a child within.

You know, your dreams of childhood, like the dreams of my friends, are there for you. Perhaps, like my second friend, though, they have become buried beneath layers of doubt, not unlike layers of seashore sand.

Change Your World

Can you visualize yourself standing before the ocean, a soft breeze blowing about you? Can you visualize the wind lifting, blowing the sand in all directions, revealing a fresh layer of sand? Try it.

Now, see yourself blowing away your layers of doubt and finding your dream, still intact. You may see it through different eyes. Its design and its dimensions may have changed but it's the same dream of your yesterday.

Do you want to activate your dream? Do you want to set it in motion? Then, you must MOVE to make it your reality. "Move" is a powerful word. It has only four letters, but look what it can do for you. Build upon the following ideas. They can only move you in the direction of your dream.

M . . . Make a mental image of your dream.

O . . . . Open the door to your dream. Bring it into your consciousness and out into the open by telling friends and loved ones about it.

V . . . . Ventilate—breathe life into your dream.

E . . . . Experience your dream. Do something to make it real for you.

One, Two, Three — GO!

Comedian Steve Allen has, about his home, many different tape recorders—one for each project on which he is working. He also has a three point plan. You could call it his "pyramid plan," for achieving his dreams and desires.

First he visualizes an idea, then he creates a plan for achieving that dream and finally he acts upon his plan. This is when he records his thoughts on tape, making them a reality.

You, too, can design your pyramid plan for making your dreams come true. Call it "One, Two Three — GO!" Think. Plan. Act.

But, before you can find your dream, you must give yourself permission to do so. You must stand back from your present life—still your mind and ask yourself what you really want to do with the rest of your life.

You must free yourself from criticism—from forces both inside and outside your being. You must build your self confidence, never forgetting you are unique and there is no one else exactly like you. And then, you must begin to think and act creatively.

On Target

Anybody who has been twelve years old surely can remember times of laughter and sharing with friends. I recall walking and talking with several girlfriends. Would we have boyfriends; would we get married; would we go to college; what kind of job would we have? I said that I was going to get married and have two children, and I was going to be a singer, an actress and a teacher. This was my dream! But this was not to come true in total for some time.

It wasn't until after I became a wife and mother that I began to pursue my other dreams. Something deep inside me reached a conscious level. My first step was to enroll in English 1A at Pasadena City College and soon after that I began singing in a choir.

A few years have passed since that time. My children are grown and I completed English 1A and moved on.

And yes, I believe my arrow has hit its mark. Focus on YOUR target, take careful aim and go for it!

Dr. Paul E. Torrance, social scientist and professor emeritus in the Department of Educational Psychology at the University of Georgia, calls being creative the process of not only becoming sensitive to your problems, your deficiencies, the gaps in your knowledge, the missing elements in your life, and even your disharmonies, but finding and testing solutions for what is missing and what is not right and then communicating the results to those about you.

Don't forget to let all your past and present experiences play a part in your journey toward your dream. Take in the sights around you. Listen to the sounds of the cities and of nature, and allow others who believe in you to help you achieve the life you are dreaming of for yourself.

Begin to keep a journal, too. Talk to yourself through the power of your written words. Let your thoughts flow, in no order or context, through your pen. Help yourself, in this way, to find out who you really are and who you want to become.

Write about the things in life you find especially interesting, then begin to act upon your thoughts, making them your realities. For, as John A. B. McLeish writes in his book, *The Ulyssean Adult* (McGraw Hill, Ryerson, Ltd., Canada), "Nothing can equal or replace the personal journal as the sphere of action for your continuing quest of the self."

Playing Out Your Dream

Sometimes you may even feel, as you chase your dream, the things you are doing are of no importance or value, because as you begin to think and act creatively, you won't have the feeling you are working. You will find, perhaps, you are working harder and longer than ever before, but there is a new excitement—an excitement unlike anything you have ever before experienced.

Another friend of mine, a designer of fine women's clothing, began, just a few years ago, to create beautiful silk screened fabrics. She then turned the rumpus room of her family home into a sewing room to change the bolts of fabric into ladies' wearing apparel. Their pool table became her cutting table. Her well used sewing machine became the vehicle for binding the cut pieces together into skirts, tops and dresses now being sold in specialty shops and in a major department store chain across the United States.

In addition, she owns two shops in her home city where she displays and sells her creations. She has a staff of at least 10 and she tells me she has never worked so hard at playing in all her life. Her world is consumed by her work, yet she does not consider it to be work. At a time when many women her age are content to drink tea and play bridge, she is following the dream of her high school days.

Dust off your long forgotten dreams. Don't let

them die with age. Create new life within yourself by finding a way to make your ideals for yourself become your realities.

Dr. Frank Crane, author of *Four Minute Essays* (Wm. H. Wise & Co., NY), said, "The greatest sin against yourself is having a good impulse and not acting upon it...Nothing is so injurious as to play with high ideals and not put them to work."

There are risks involved in changing your life—in moving from what we call our "comfort zone" into the unknown world of our desires. But don't be afraid to take those risks. For, as an anonymous poet wrote:

....the greatest hazard in life is to risk nothing.
The person who risks nothing,
does nothing, has nothing, and is nothing.
He may avoid suffering and sorrow
But he simply cannot learn, feel, change,
grow, love, live—
Only a person who risks is free.

Watch the children of our world playing in the park, pondering in their sand boxes and lazily plucking the dandelions from the grasses. Learn from them. Stop your clock. Relax. Reassess your life. Bring out the child within you—the one waiting in the wings to perform—just for you.

Sizing Up Your Dreams

I recall once receiving a beautiful pink sweater for my birthday. I excitedly pulled it over my head. But it was so big! The sleeves were so long I couldn't even see my hands. My mother rolled it up at the waist, turned up the sleeves several times, stood back smiling, and said, "You'll grow into it."

Well, maybe at different times in your life your dreams were too big for you. Why not try them on again for size—they just might fit.

Remember well your childhood visions
Ideas, thoughts, laughs and schemes
They're not gone
They're just forgotten
Breathe deep
Recall
Relive the Dreams...

Shake your dreams loose. Breathe life into them—

Dream on...

Dream on...

Dream on...

"Far away there in the sunshine are my highest aspirations. I may not reach them,but I can look up and see their beauty, believe in them, and try to follow where they lead."

- Louisa May Alcott.

Thoughts on Health & Humor

"It is necessary to try to surprise one's self always; this occupation ought to last as long as life."

- Queen Christina

"The ideals which have lighted my way, and time after time given me new courage to face life cheerfully have been kindness, beauty and truth."

- Albert Einstein

Don't refuse to go on an ocasional wild goose chase; that's what wild geese are made for."

- Henry S. Haskins

Your Thoughts on Health & Humor

Larry Rich
Affordable Attractions Alliance
209 Reiber Road
Renfrew, PA 16053
(412) 482-2944

Larry Rich

You probably know Larry Rich from major circus, stage and television appearances. His credits include over three decades in circus arenas in Europe and America, most recently with Le Cirque Universal in Canada. Stage and television performances have built a broad base of appeal to audiences of all ages.

Equally at home in smart supper clubs, conventions, fairs, or the circus tanbark, Larry's comedy delights every type of audience.

Always in good taste and always entertaining, Larry Rich blends his humor into one of the most energetic, laugh provoking, and appealing shows on the market today. His format is as varied as his audience. Whether as banquet speaker, seminar leader, master of ceremonies or circus clown, Larry keeps the show moving with his quick wit and seasoned timing.

His growing list of credits reflect his increasing popularity and expanding talents. A few recent highlights include: Ringmaster - Shrine Circus Cow Palace, San Francisco, CA; Master of Ceremonies - Pacific Northern Exposition, Vancouver, British Columbia; Producing Clown - Hoxie Bros Circus; Convention appearances for major U.S. Corporations; scores of state, regional and county fairs; and many special appearances throughout the U.S. and Canada.

This promises to be a banner year for this talented, versatile comedy performer. His dedication to laughter and his wide experience in television, commercials and live performances can only lead to increasing success and a place of his own among the true comedy stars of the entertainment world.

Clowning—
the Art and the Profession

By Larry Rich

"Men have been wise in very different modes,
but they have always laughed the same way."
- Samuel Johnson

Probably the most interesting and underplayed element of the circus is the place I called home for about twenty years, "Clown Alley." There really is such a place in every circus. It's not just a figment of some publicist's imagination. In the days of "tent circus" the Clown Alley was near the performer's entrance, known as the "Backdoor" so the clowns could make their quick costume changes, and be back in the "big top" in case of an emergency. In later years there was a small separate tent set up for the clown's dressing room, and still called "Clown Alley."

There's an unwritten law, if you aren't a clown you don't go near "Clown Alley" because these practical jokers might play a prank on you. Personally, I had more fun playing jokes on other clowns in the alley. I used to hide hand props, hang wigs up high out of reach, or rig a water bucket over the door sill, so the next person in would get a "free shower."

Circus Magic

The magic of the circus has never grown old, to the media, or to me, and never will. Spend two and one half hours in front of circus clowns, and their gags can do wonders for a tired housewife or frazzled businessman. Most people think they are bringing the kids to the circus because it will make them happy, and it will.

The way it really works is the minute they sit down, the clowns start working "come-in," as patrons are being seated prior to the performance. These clowns are there to "warm-up" the crowd...let down their hair, and enjoy the show that's coming up. Suddenly, the businessman is laughing harder than the youngsters.

The cares of the day sort of evaporate as they start to snicker—this laughter is contagious, and soon it bursts into guffaws and "belly laughs." From stock broker to dirt farmer, from duty nurse to scrub lady, from teacher to salesperson—all are equal and their laughter fills the "big top."

Today, with most circuses working the huge arenas and other buildings, that mystic of the circus "Big Top" is lost and the excitement comes in a different way, with thrilling high acts, dangerous wild animals, and modern theatrical lighting effects...still the Clowns ply their comedy in the age-old way, evoking laughter through outrageous costumes, clever gags, and broad gestures.

The First Joey

Joseph Grimaldi, perhaps the greatest clown in circus history, was born in 1779 and died in 1837. He was the creator of the English clown, and the first of a long line of "Joeys." In my early days, I called my clown character "JO-JO" because, in his day Joseph Grimaldi was the best...and, I wanted to be twice as good in my day...hence, JO-JO. In the late 60's there were many amateur clowns using the JO-JO name, and it became difficult to get bookings, so I buried a set of wardrobe, including big shoes in my backyard in Ohio...thus burying JO-JO...and emerging as "Circus Clown Larry Rich," something no one could steal.

After all, many of my circus clown friends used their own name, so I felt comfortable with it.

No two clowns are exactly alike. Each Joey creates his own facial makeup and costume design. These are morally copyrighted.

Clown Character

Basically there are three types of clowns—Whiteface, Auguste, and the only true American clown the Tramp or Hobo character .

The Whiteface clown applies a coat of white makeup over his entire face, neck, and ears and powders it with talc powder to set the makeup, and keep it from smearing off on his clothing. Then his colorful, comical designs are drawn on with grease pencils. The Whiteface clown usually has a bright costume, with a ruffle around the neck. Possibly the most famous modern day Whiteface clown is Ronald McDonald of hamburger fame.

The Auguste, or European clown is known for his big bulbous nose, big shoes, baggy clothes...often getting hit with water, or smacked on the rump with a "slap-stick." Broad visual comedy is often referred to as "Slap-stick Comedy," because this prop is used to hit another clown, making a loud noise...while not really hurting the victim. He grabs and rubs his rear-end as though the pain was unbearable. We laugh at that pain because it happened to someone else. We think it's funny when somebody else gets hurt, but not when we do . Other variations of the Auguste clown are midgets, dwarfs, and men dressed as women.

Clown/Comedian

There is a great deal of difference between a clown and a comedian. Today you are aquainted with many comedians on television, in movies, and night clubs. A comedian operates on one, and only one emotion—LAUGHTER, using his voice. As a clown, we seek all the emotions, laughter, sorrow, pity, grief, pain, etc. The clown must be adept at all of these and to evoke them we use gestures and the voice. Pantomime is essential in the circus, where the audience is often too far away to hear what's said without a microphone, or in situations where we don't speak the language.

There are very few real clowns, but many imitations. Most of the so-called funny men are poor clowns who overdo their emoting with a lot of action and weak facial contortions. A real clown is very subtle and can do more with a raised eyebrow, or tilt of his head, than all of the grimaces there are. As you might remember, there were some great old-time clowns, such as: Charlie Chaplin, Buster Keaton, W.C. Fields, Victor Borge, Ben Blue, and Red Skelton.

As my friend, Danny Chapman said, "Clowns are in the greatest demand but the entertainment industry is swamped with comedians and imitation clowns."

Clowns in the form of court jesters have brought love and laughter to heads of state. Some of the more famous men in history were clowns at heart. In his philosophy, a clown can see the unimportance of the individual person in the overall scheme of things. A clown looks for the humor in all things—he can't always see it, but he looks for it anyway. If he looks hard enough, long enough, usually he'll find something funny in every situation.

Managing Stress with Fun

It's the little things in life that bother us! For example, you can sit on a mountain top, but you can't sit on a tack.

Today there is a lot of talk about stress...stress management, reducing stress in the workplace, even stress workshops. The way I get out of stressful situations is to look for something funny in the situation. That's not always easy. Most of the time we get so caught up in the stress of a given task, that we bring on more stress by worrying about whatever the job is we're stressed out with in the first place.

Here's what I do. I look at the stressful situation with both eyes wide open...looking beyond the job at hand to the completed task, seeing myself enjoying the reward or glory in doing the right thing...and usually there's something funny that hits me...a laugh emerges, and soon I've calmed myself enough to attack whatever is creating the stress.

A teacher in high school once told our class, when we were working on a report, "Beginning is half-done." His meaning didn't sink in until many years later. Putting off the start of a project causes stress. Beginning even the slightest little effort is the hardest part. The procrastination holds back the creative juices, and stress sets in.

The Heart of Clowning

I've been called upon to do comedy workshops on clowning, and I strongly emphasize that I can teach you how to put on makeup, and how to make a clown wordrobe, and build props...but the one thing I can't teach you is —HOW TO BE FUNNY. That's something you've got to develop from within. Real clowning comes from the heart. It isn't something you can read in a book and go out tomorrow and do. It takes practice...with all kinds of audiences, under all kinds of situations to put the clown "under fire" and temper his timing like fire tempers steel, making it strong for its intended purpose.

I'm thankful for those thousands of people across America and in 17 foreign countries that laughed while I practiced my craft. In my early days on the Mills Brothers Circus as a clown, I worked hard, watching the other acts, developing my own sense of timing that spells the difference between a chuckle and a laugh.

Fortunately, I've always been a "people watcher"...and saw humor in a lot of "real-life situations"...these were the basis for many of my routines.

Recently, there have been a lot of small signs appearing in automobiles saying, "Baby on Board." This spawned a "walk-around" gag of a doll baby on a plank, on my shoulder, with a big yellow sign under the doll that says, "BABY ON BOARD." A simple, but funny bit, with limited props.

A more complex gag is the "Clown Car" with about twenty clowns inside...there's no trap-door, just a very crowded situation for the participants. The car's seats are all removed, so that the gutted car has a large compartment from the dash all the way to the back of the trunk. The rule is simple—last one in—first one out, and so on, until all of the clowns are out of the car, cavorting around the ring. Then the last clown out, usually a midget cop, chases all of the clowns out of the arena. Most of the classic clown gags end in a chase...others with a huge bang! Personally I never liked loud explosions because I thought it scared more kids than it made laugh. As clowns we're there to get laughs, not scare the wits out of our audience.

At the circus, clowns offer the comic relief to some very tense moments, where daredevils flirt with death. As in life, there can only be so much tension before we need to laugh. On the other hand, the dangerous acts offer pace for the comedy of circus clowns.

P. T. Barnum is purported to have said, "Clowns and elephants are the pegs that the circus hangs on." There are some small circuses that don't have an elephant, but none without a clown.

From Clown to Consultant

From the circus to the television studio was a natural progression for me since my high school days. Involvement with Junior Achievement's Radio Company sponsored by our local radio station sparked an interest in broadcasting. During my Navy days in Norfolk, Virginia, I was co-host of a popular children's show. This led to numerous radio and TV commercial jobs, as a clown and straight announcer. Upon release from the Navy I returned to circus for the rest of the summer, then into broadcasting full time for nearly 12 years. From DJ, newscaster, to sales and management.

While on top in a local market, I stepped off the solid ground, and went back "on the road" to my first love, clowning at fairs, festivals, celebrations, and special events. This started out as a strolling act, later evolved into a stage act of magic and balloon sculpture. My previous knowledge and ability in marketing increased my worth to fair managers, because they got an act and a publicity campaign that sold tickets for one price.

This was a fun project for several years, parlaying into our very successful Affordable Attractions Alliance, a talent production firm producing over 300 shows at fairs and festivals annually.

From clown to consultant in 33 years of cheers and laughter, these days we're spending a lot of time consulting sales and marketing people in how to "Bill it like a Circus."

The tools change, people don't! Audiences still laugh at the same ridiculous stuff they did thirty years ago...only MY TIMING is better today!

Besides stockbrokers, talent agents are probably the best telephone sales people, dealing with clients everyday on the phone, increasing our skills and worth to our clients in telemarketing techniques that work!

I'm reminded of an old gag that involved one of those huge "Texas Phones" and an Ace bandage. A clown would dash into the arena with a "Long distance call for Larry Rich." I would rush out to take it, shout into the phone, "Hello-Hello-Hello." The other clown would then take the end of the elastic bandage, and stretch it between my legs, behind me. I'd ask the operator to give it to me. He would let the elastic snap, and I'd fall forward in a heap, to big laughs.

Amateur Clowns

In recent years there has been a real surge in amateur clown groups, and fraternal clowns. Some of these non—professionals are very funny, and do charity work at hospitals and parades. But many of these groups unintentionally are putting the working professional clown out of work by doing personal appearances for little or no money. Even major circus producers are finding that good clowns can't compete with the amateurs. Like many of America's craftsmen, a cheaper, inferior product has come on the clown scene.

There are gimmicks, like "Clown College," run by the Ringling Brothers, Barnum & Bailey Circus, in Venice, Florida. Basically, this is a publicity stunt in each town the circus plays. To get media coverage, they'll hold an open "audition" for Clown College. The local TV covers this, and feature stories are written about possible candidates.

Though most of these so-called graduates are very capable, competent individuals in make-up, costume design, juggling, stilt-walking etc., most of them lack the key ingrediant to being a successful professional clown...they aren't funny.

I remember when I was just twelve years old, and I called an agent in Florida about working with a circus during the coming summer months. I had sent pictures, newspaper clippings, and a letter to his office, and was following up my mailing with the phone call. The agent asked me,"Do you juggle?" I said "NO." He asked, "Do you ride a unicycle?" I replied, "NO." He asked, "Do you walk on stilts?" Again I said, "NO." He said in frustration, "Just what do you do?" I calmly said, "I make people laugh, isn't that what a clown's supposed to do?" There was a long silence, then the agent responded by saying, "Yes, and I wish there were more FUNNY CLOWNS these days."

I got the job, and have always held it in high regard, that I was able to get laughs. Even today, with the simplest of props and facial expressions, I can get laughs.

Keep Getting Up

Though I've moved on from the circus into other avenues of clowning, my days with the circus gave me the background for taking a fall...getting up, laughing it off, and going on with whatever it is I choose to do. A wise old clown once said,"It's funny to fall down. It's not funny if you don't get back up." Whether you're a clown or not, this is good advice.

Success is the journey, not the destination. It doesn't matter how many times you fall down.

What matters is, *that you keep getting back up.*

Thoughts on Health & Humor

"There are three things which are real—
God, human folly and laughter.
The first two are beyond our comprehension.
So we must do what we can with the third."
- John F. Kennedy

"He who would be healthy, let him be cheerful."
- Welsh Proverb

"Humor has justly been regarded
as the finest perfection of poetic genius."
- Carlyle

Your Thoughts on Health & Humor

Gittle Langner Saks, O.M.D., C.A.
10573 W. Pico Blvd., #217
Los Angeles, CA 90064
(213) 271-8851

Dr. Gittle Langner Saks

Gittle Langner Saks, O.M.D., C.A., is a Doctor of Oriental Medicine in private practice in West Lost Angeles. Her successful holistic health clinic proudly displays a testimonial to Dr. Saks' services from the famous movie actor Gene Hackman.

Dr. Saks has been involved in the field of holistic health since 1963. As a primary health care practitioner she is dedicated to helping people overcome pain, relieve stress and tension and look and feel better.

Her schooling included two years of college in Toronto, Canada, after which she continued her studies in Los Angeles and earned her doctorate in Oriental Medicine at the California Acupuncture College.

She was at the forefront in the fight for legislation for California acupuncture schools to be recognized. Her background includes teaching, lecturing and writing in the holistic health field. She has lectured at the University of Illinois Medical School and has been a volunteer at Turnaround, an acupuncture clinic, primarily treating homeless drug addicts.

Since 1985 Dr. Saks has hosted the Los Angeles AM radio show, "In Search of Health", on station KIEV. She is successful in helping people quit smoking in just three visits. Personal injury accidents, workers' compensation, slenderizing treatments, T.M.J. problems and pain problems are no problem at the clinic. She has patients purring like a kitten with foot reflexology treatments. Other services include acupuncture, acupressure, therapeutic exercises, nutrition, herbal and homeopathic drugless prescriptions.

Dr. Saks' well-established reputation as a Doctor of Oriental Medicine is unique in that she is licensed for many years in the State of California as an acupuncturist, electrologist, cosmetician and message therapist.

How to Energize Yourself:
Movement for Meridian Energy Balance

By Gittle Langner Saks, O.M.D., C.A.

"Be good to your body. It's the only one you have."
- Gittle Langner Saks

I frequently refer to myself as an excellent holistic health practitioner. My expertise in the health field is probably due to my own health problems as well as the fact that my forefathers were great faith healers in Europe. I must have inherited some of their unique talent and expanded it by trusting my own intuition and developing practical methods to help myself and others overcome illness and maintain better health.

The sages of ancient times emphasized NOT the treatment of disease, but rather the prevention of its occurrence.

Energy Channels

An important key to good health is keeping our lines or "energy" channels, the meridians of our body, in balance.

I sometimes describe "energy" as a straight line on the highway. First, picture a straight line going down the highway. Then, picture a highway with short lines and spaces. Fill in the white spaces to make a straight highway line. Another analogy: lines of energy perhaps look like invisible wires.

When you turn on your radio, the sound coming from the station, for instance KIEV, is traveling on an invisible line of energy. If you hear static it means you're not hearing a good energy. It may be too loud, or too soft...or you may not hear the sound at all. What you want to hear is good energy and good sound.

Picture two glasses of water: one three-quarters full, and the other one-third full. If we wanted to equalize the amount or balance the amount in both glasses we would "add" water to the glass that is one-third full. In holistic health we stimulate the energy line which is deficient.

How to Energize

"How to Energize Yourself: Movement for Meridian Energy Balance" is based on the acupuncture concept of meridians or channels which contain the flow of "chi" or body energy. For diagnostic purposes, Oriental Health scrutinizes twelve different lines of energy. I diagnose these various lines of energy in the body when a patient comes to the clinic.

I determine the state of the twelve primary channels of energy by evaluating the pulse. We have six main pulses on the left hand and six on the right. I then proceed to diagnose the tongue. Both the tongue and the pulse reveal various internal conditions.

All energy lines should be kept in balance as much as possible. Lung energy, large intestine energy, and liver energy, representing three energy lines, affect those organs. When an energy line is out of balance, for instance the liver energy, it does not necessarily mean the organ, "liver," has a problem. It doesn't mean one should go running to the doctor complaining, "there's something wrong with my liver."

In Oriental Medicine, "eyesight" is synonymous with "liver energy." Acupuncturists, including myself, always treat liver energy when treating eye problems.

Just as we must balance and maintain good energy, it's important not to absorb negative, or what acupuncturists refer to as "evil" or "perverse" energy from entering our bodies. When we touch someone, or give a body massage or foot reflexology massage, it is important to brush that negative energy off our hands. One way is to clap the hands together in an up and down motion. Washing the hands after physical contact also removes negativity.

The following illustration goes back many years to when I was studying massage; a patient came in with pain in the right shoulder blade or scapula area. A couple of hours after he left, I noticed a severe pain in my right shoulder blade. When I mentioned the incident in class the following day the instructor asked me if I knew how to protect myself. "Don't you know how to shake off negative vibrations from your hands?" I learned quickly, but too often forgot to apply the correct principles.

Saving Energy

Besides stimulating energy we can save energy. One of my patients asked, "Don't you know anything else I can do to save my energy?" I replied that I frequently wear a magnetic belt. I believe many people are not aware of the therapeutic value of magnets. The magnetic belt has tiny pockets to hold small magnets. Wearing the magnetic belt is protection against absorbing negative energy.

With regard to losing energy or health, I am reminded of the fascinating story involving my Mother's Grandfather who was a great healer in Europe. When

I was a little girl, an old lady by the name of Mrs. Rosenberg used to visit us frequently. She walked with much difficulty and always complained that she wasn't quite well.

Mrs. Rosenberg filled my young ears with the story about how she travelled by horse and wagon to visit the Chenchiner Rabbi, who was my great Grandfather, in order to get his blessing for good health. The Rabbi handed her four cubes of sugar, advising her to take one immediately, one sugar cube when she entered the coach, and the other two when she returned home. Mrs. Rosenberg insisted that she followed the Rabbi's instructions until she got off the coach, where she met a friend. "Where are you going?" inquired Mrs. Rosenberg. "I'm not well," replied her friend, "I'm travelling to the Rabbi for his healing and blessings."

Mrs. Rosenberg responded, "I'll save you the trip; the good Rabbi just gave me his blessings and advised me how to take four lumps of sugar for a complete healing. You know what, I'll give you two of my sugar lumps."

Mrs. Rosenberg's health improved a little but she never recovered completely. She returned to the Rabbi some months later. As she entered the doorway, Mrs. Rosenberg was stunned as the good Rabbi said, "Stupid woman, *when someone gives you a blessing or remedy, you don't give half your health away*. You will live to be very old. As a matter of fact you will have added years, but you will never be completely well. You gave away a part of your health."

I recall Mrs Rosenberg surviving her children, and living to be a centenarian.

Negative Vibrations

Another method of keeping negative vibrations from entering the body is one that Orientals have kept secret. It's the correct placement of the tongue. Two very important lines of energy are the line of energy that runs up the center on the front of our body, and the line of energy, on the opposite side, running straight up the back. These two invisible lines of energy connect close to under the tongue. In order to maintain a balance of energy, we connect these two different lines by keeping our tongue on the roof of the mouth or palate. The "normal" resting posture for the tongue is on the roof of the mouth. Ironically the normal resting posture for the tongue coincides with the point that joins the two extraordinary lines of energy in the front and back of the body.

Interestingly enough this ties in closely with the T.M.J. (Temporamandibular Joint) problem and the energy balance of the face. Most people are unaware of having an abnormal resting posture of the tongue until they have a neck ache, shoulder ache, or facial pain. Other abnormal resting posture symptoms of the facial muscles and tongue are mal-occlusion, mouth-breathing, and teeth gnashing or grinding.

In most cases when you have an abnormal mouth posture, the roof of the mouth is too high. This happens all too frequently when an infant isn't nursed. It is compounded by sucking a bottle. The roof of an infant's mouth is very soft. An artificial nipple grooves into the roof of the mouth forcing the palate higher and higher.

We also aggravate this problem by putting noxious objects into the mouth. A thumb, pencils, or any instrument, all noxious objects, will cause the palate and occlusion to become abnormal.

When the tongue is in the wrong place behind the teeth, banging against the teeth, it knocks them out of alignment. Our tongue exerts tremendous pressure against our teeth, as we swallow twice a minute when awake and once a minute when asleep. Only in rare cases will the tongue not cause problems when resting behind the teeth. There are exercises that help in maintaining and retraining the mouth to normalize and balance the facial muscles and their energy.

How do some people deal with the extremely bad habits of bruxing, or teeth grinding, and gnashing, which can lead to mal-occlusion, T.M.J. problems and headaches? In the Philippines, for instance, it can be stopped very easily, by smacking the unaware teeth gnasher across the mouth and teeth when they are hard at work gnashing. But the teeth grinder must be smacked with a slipper. They believe that if you were to use your hand, the bad habit would transfer to you.

Exercise and Total Body Movement for Energy Balance

Begin with a nice good stretch to increase your vital energy. Get up on your feet and stretch upwards, reach up and take a part of the sky, stretch and stretch some more with your hands higher and higher. Now shake out your hands. Give them a good shake. Stretching is a great way to energize.

Another movement to help balance the energy is self-massage. Important massage points are found around the wrists. There are many acupuncturists who ONLY insert needles around the wrists and ankles. By massaging around the wrists, we affect many energy lines. The lung energy line is in a line with the thumb on the palm side of the hand. Moving inward on the palm side of the wrist above the middle finger, we pass the pericardium line. This energy affects relaxation of the chest and diaphragm. If you're nauseous or seasick on a cruise, there are little rubber bands with a button which are available. Pressed on the pericardium line, these accupressure buttons will stop nausea and relax the chest. Massaging around the wrist not only affects the lung line but also various other energy lines including the heart. Shortness of breath, relaxing the chest, nausea and balance are benefitted by this massage movement. By massaging vigorously around the wrists and tips of the fingers, you stimulate the area where an exchange of energy takes place. Use firm, penetrating pressure to give yourself a good massage and enhance the energy flow in your body.

Why do Chinese and Japanese kimonos have extra large sleeves? We say the Orientals are busy at work giving their wrists a good acupressure massage underneath those wide sleeves. Just like the Orientals, today many people have discovered the joy of a good wrist and hand massage. It feels great; and so does ankle and foot massage. You may have heard of foot reflexology massage and its benefits. Not only does the massage feel good but it is beneficial in balancing energy lines. All toes have specific therapeutic benefits when massaged. You will soon discover this as you learn you can even remove a nagging headache by vigorously massaging your big toe. It is interesting to note that the different lines of energy change direction as they flow toward the tips of the toes.

Energizing the Heart Channel

It is my theory that orchestra conductors frequently live to their late nineties because they are constantly exercising the heart channel. A good exercise to stimulate the heart line is swinging your arms as though you are leading an orchestra. You might try this exercise. Swing your arms up and down and to the sides. Sing as you exercise. In my lecture at the Pasadena Convention Center, I noticed the crew who were televising my talk were also participating in these exercises. Swing your arms up and down and up to the ceiling and across to the side of the room, and give yourself a good clap. It's good for your heart to clap your hands. Clapping affects your heart line because the heart channel ends in the center of the palm.

I refer to this next movement as waddling like a duck. There is a spot on the heart meridian or channel under the arm that is very sensitive to the touch. Place your thumbs just beneath the armpit with the elbows at right angles, straight out to the sides. Bring the elbows up and down continuing to give that armpit a really vigorous massage. Any movements which involve swinging your arms are beneficial for energizing the heart channel.

The following movement which benefits the heart line can be done even while sitting in your chair. It is the swinging of your arms and pitching ball. Vigorously pitch an imaginary ball. Throw your ball right across the room. Pitch and pitch. Now reverse arms and gain speed pitching. Continue this exercise to the count of eight for each arm. Remember, it's good for your heart.

Laughter as Exercise

Another great exercise is laughter. Laughter is one of the best exercises we do for vitality and healing. A good strong belly laugh is most important.

Laughter makes you feel good. It's excellent therapy for patients who have a life threatening illness. When lecturing about health and laughter I have someone from the audience tell a joke. Everybody then forces laughter for about five minutes.

The following is a true story related to health that would be an example of a joke told at this time. My family was listening to the news the other evening when the news commentator announced they had just discovered that AIDS could be transmitted by oral sex. The announcer mentioned that this was unknown before. My mother, who is eighty seven and can't hear out of one ear and wears a hearing aid in the other said, "EGGS! You hear that, he said that eggs are good for you. I eat two eggs every morning for breakfast. They just said on television eggs are healthy for you."

Beauty

This chapter would not be complete without movements for the face and beauty. There are many facial acu-points that can be stimulated for beauty. I teach a technique which I developed that involves using your fingernails, instead of massaging the face with only the fingertips. Your nails add a little more stimulus than fingertips when they massage your skin.

Massage around your eyebrows. It's invigorating.

Then move from the center of the forehead, massaging towards the outer edge of the eyebrow. Starting at the top of the hairline, with your fingernails coming down to the side of both eyes, then under the eye on the orbital ridge, circle the eye. Repeat this movement several times. We can do this same fingernail massage movement around the lips. Starting beneath the nose at the filtrum, using your fingernails ever so lightly, go around the lips, with a light scratchy movement. Come up to the ear lobe and now move down to the chin line and up to the ear lobe again. This should make you feel kind of tingly.

Wake up!

A frequently asked question is, "What can I do if I find myself falling asleep at the wheel?" The following exercise movement works to revive you although it might look a little wierd, especially to other drivers. But it works! Pull your hair. Pull it hard! It'll wake you up. Yank your hair as hard as you can.

Another wakeup exercise that's good for boredom syndrome is the "thymus thumper." The thymus is beneath the two bones at the base of the neck. I was reminded of this exercise at a seminar I was attending. A female teacher of retarded children told me about one child, a boy of nine, who was always falling asleep in class. She was bewildered and determined to do something. "How do I keep this child awake?"

Then she remembered her studies about thumping the thymus. She taught the young boy to "punch, and thump your awake button." He has never fallen asleep in class since.

Breath of Life Exercise

I consider breathing exercises most important. One of the best exercises to really help with your breathing and the line of energy which integrates the upper, middle and lower functions of the body is called the "breath of fire" or "breath of life." In doing this exercise it is important to remember that as you inhale you expand your rib cage and as you exhale you contract.

Visualize a balloon. Think of, or picture a balloon as you inhale and exhale. When air is pumped into the balloon it expands; when it's deflated the balloon contracts. With this visualization in mind place both thumbs on your ribs as your fingers push in your stomach and diaphragm while you exhale. Unfortunately most people do this wrong the first time. It's inhale, expand. Exhale, deflate or contract. Start slowly and gradually increase the speed. Rapidly inhale and exhale. Remember, you're using your nails to push as you exhale. There are many vital organs at the upper stomach or diaphragm, and some very important acupuncture points in that area. By using your fingernails instead of the pads of your fingers to push, you'll get a very good stimulation. This exercise should be done with a powerful breath. The more you put into it, the more you get out of it. Take in a deep breath, and hold the breath, inhale, and hold the breath some more. As you breathe out, squeeze all your organs. Squeeze your chest, your diaphragm, your stomach. Squeeze your sexual organs and your anus, and relax. This exercise is very good for getting your whole body going.

The yogas believe this exercise increases life expectancy. They claim that each series of breaths counts for only one breath. They also claim, as many religions do, that when we're born it's pre-determined how many breaths our life will be. They further say our life span will be increased by the amount of "breath of life" exercise series we do.

After doing the "Breath of Life" exercise a good movement to continue with is "tense and relax." You're not holding anything....only a good thought.

Start by tensing your toes. Tense your toes some more. Tense your ankles. Now tense your calves. Keep tensing as you tense your legs. Squeeze hard. Tense your diaphragm, your buttocks, up to the top of your back and neck. Now tense your shoulders. While tensing I want you to tense your hands into little fists, and now your forearms, elbows and upper arms. Squeeze. Now go to the face area, pucker your lips and nose, squeeze them as you squeeze your eyes closed. Squeeze your face into a prune. Squeeze your ears. You can squeeze your ears by squeezing your neck a little more. Squeeze your whole body. Really squeeze, and while you're holding this position keep a good thought. Stay in this position.

Now we're going to relax. I want you to start with your toes and relax them slowly. Relax the calves, and coming up the legs relax your hips. Relax your chest. Slowly relax your buttocks, your back, come up to the top of your back to your neck. See how good it feels. Relax your shoulders, shake them gently, as you experience your back relaxing. Your hands and your arms are now loosening up and so is your chin. Think of your chin and your lips as you slowly relax your nose, eyes, ears and face. Feels good doesn't it? Shake your body loosely. Give yourself a good shake from head to toe. Shaking is good for your body. It feels good to be completely relaxed.

Energize the Eyes

Our eyes also fatigue and need special attention. We can energize our eyes. Start by rubbing your palms together; rub, rub, rub. Build up a good static electricity. After you have built up the static electricity in your hands put the palms of your hands across your eyes. Hold them there and slowly count to six. Repeat the movement and rub your hands together. Again place your hands across your eyes. This time open and close your eyes; flutter your eyelids. Be aware of the fluttering against the palms of your hands. This movement is excellent for tired eyes.

Neck Exercises

Many people have problems with their neck, such as a stiff neck or a whiplash. These movements for the neck are called resistance movements. Before you start, observe the four walls around you; the two to the sides, in front and back.

You are going to put the right side of your head through the right wall. At the same time you will resist with your right hand. With your right hand resting about an inch above your right ear, push the right side of your head through the right wall. Your right hand is going to resist as you push your head to the right. Count to six while pushing. Now relax to the count of six. Repeat this movement. Change hands and with your left hand on the left side of your head, push the left side of your head to the left wall. Your left hand is going to resist as your head pushes to the left. Count to six while pushing. Now relax to the count of six. Repeat this movement. I practice my Spanish counting with these exercises. I repeat uno, dos, tres, quatro, cinco, seis. Relax, two, three, four, five, six. It is important for your normal mouth posture that your chin be parallel with the floor. Keeping your chin tilted forward will cause undue stress on the neck.

Following through with resistance movements, with either hand on your forehead, try to move your forehead toward the wall in front of you; resist with your hand on your forehead as you push your forehead back. Count to six moving forward, and then count to six as you relax. Repeat the movements twice.

Now you are going to push the back of your head to the wall behind you. Using both hands place your fingertips and fingernails into the base of your skull; it will give you a good invigorating feeling. With the hands below the occipital, and your chin down, direct your head to the wall behind you, using your hands to resist as your hands push your neck and head. At the same time your fingers are massaging the base of your skull. It's another form of acupressure with your fingernails.

The next movement in this series is "traction." You're going to maneuver your head as close as you can to the sky. No hands are used. Remember, your head is like a ball on an axis ; your chin is parallel with the floor. You want to push the top of your head right through the ceiling. Again stretch to the count of six, then relax to the count of six. Remember your head is moving upwards from the back of your neck. After doing this series of movements your neck should feel marvelous.

Low Back Pain

According to statistics, eighty percent of the population will have a problem with their lower back during their lifetime. The following exercise movements will help.

The following movement can be done the lazy way,

either in a chair, or on a mat on the floor. While sitting in a chair bring your right foot up and place it on the chair as you count to six. Set your right foot down on the floor again counting to six. Repeat the movement and then switch to your left foot. Bring your left foot on to the chair to the count of six, then follow through the same as you did with your right foot. Now bring both feet on to the chair, count to six; place feet on the floor, again count from one to six. Repeat the movement with both feet.

This next one is easy. With both legs straight out in front of you while sitting in your chair, point your toes in. Count from one to six. Relax your toes to the count of six, and repeat the movement.

If you really are suffering from lower back pain this exercise will open up the spaces in your low back and release the pressure between the discs.

Lie down on the floor beside your bed. Bring both legs up onto the bed, making sure that your knees are bent at a forty- five degree angle. Relax this way for about forty- five minutes.

I developed these movements to take the pressure off the low back while walking, at a time when I was confined to a wheel chair:

1. Walk slowly and deliberately.

2. First come down on the toe and then the heel.

3. Exaggerate the knee bend. Bring your knee up, and walk toe, heel.

Try the above movement while walking backwards. When walking backwards, we naturally walk toe, heel. Try walking backwards if walking up a hill is very difficult for you. When you turn around and walk forward you'll find you walk normally and your legs will swing more easily.

I am frequently asked, "What acupressure point can help relieve low back pain?" An acupuncture point most effective in eliminating back pain is behind the knee. Massage the area with your fingertips, or fingernails. You may use a pencil eraser or tip of a ballpoint pen to massage the area. It really works. I always include this point when I treat low back pain.

Once, while talking with my sister on the phone she let me know that she had a "terrible backache." I told her to get a pencil with an eraser on it and massage behind her knee while we were engaged in conversation. I then suggested, "put the eraser behind your kneecap between the tendons, in the bulge, and really massage the area." At the end of our conversation I inquired,"By the way, how's your backache? She responded, "What backache?"

I am reminded of Mr. Samuel Smith, who was having an excruciating backache, neck pain and T.M.J. facial pain. His wife took him to Dr. J., who examined Mr. Smith and asked him how he was feeling. Mr. Smith responded, "in spite of all the agonizing pain I am having, God is good to me and takes care of me." "How is that?" asked the wise Doctor. "Well, every night I wake up because of my backache. I need to urinate, and I go to the bathroom. God is very good to me and turns the light on for me when I open the door. He turns the light off for me when I'm finished. Then I go back to bed." The baffled

Doctor called Mrs. Smith into his private office and asked her what her husband meant by all this. "Oh my God!" she said, "he's urinating in the refrigerator again."

This chapter only briefly covers the subject of body "energy" movement and health, their significance and how to feel better with therapeutic exercise.

Be Good to Your Body.
It's the Only One You Have.

"The sages of ancient times emphasized not the treatment of disease, but rather, the prevention of its occurrence. To administer medicine to disease which has already developed and to suppress revolts which have already begun is comparable to the behavior of one who begins to dig a well after he has become thirsty or one who begins to forge weapons after he is engaged in battle."

\- Su Wen,
Yellow Emperor's Classics

Thoughts on Health & Humor

"Ill-Health, of body or of mind, is defeat...
Health alone is victory.
Let everyone, if they can manage it,
contrive to be healthy!"
- Sir Walter Scott

"Wrinkles should merely indicate
where smiles have been."
- Mark Twain

"Laughter is a tranquilizer with no side effects."
- Arnold H. Glasow

Your Thoughts on Health & Humor

Walter Weber
Registered Professional Entomologist
36 W. Roberts Road
Indianapolis, IN 46217
(317) 786-7251

MEMBER NATIONAL SPEAKERS ASSOCIATION

Walter Weber

Walter Weber invites you to his one hundredth birthday, January 6, 2011. No gifts please.

Walter grew up on a farm near Melvin, Illinois. He is an alumnus of the University of Illinois with a master's degree from Purdue University.

Walter spent twelve years teaching vocational agriculture, biology, and chemistry ant thirty years with the Indiana Farm Bureau Cooperative where he wrote their annual Pest Control Guide.

Walter and his wife, Eunice have carried their camera to all fifty states and several foreign countries.

After retirement he served as consultant to the Rid-A-Bird Company and E. I. DuPont Company. He has written three books on vector borne pathogens: Health Hazards from Pigeons, Starlings and English Sparrows; Diseases Transmitted by Rats and Mice; Fleas, Ticks & Cockroaches, Disease Disseminators.

He has also written two non-serious books: Humor and Fun in Signs of Your Life, *and* The Unflushables; Outhouses, History and Humor - The Hole Picture.

Walter is a member of the Indiana Academy of Science, The National Speakers Association and the Lutheran Church. He is a Registered Professional Entomologist.

Humor Makes for Happy Trails

The Humor In Your Life

By Walter Weber

Humorous signs have proved so rewarding to me that I naturally think they deserve a place all their own.
- Herb True, University of Notre Dame

Can you imagine today's world without television and humor? Pictures are the universal language. They communicate peoples's thoughts and unlock keys to the past. The oldest existing American photograph was made in 1839.

After God created Heaven and Earth he made man and woman, then in order to keep the whole thing from falling apart he invented humor.

The pictures in this chapter are from two of my books. *Signs of Life* is a collection of eye-catching signs featuring humor, laughter, and fun. Humor brings smiles. A smile is the world's best face lift and it is free. A smile fosters good will, creates happiness and is a sign of friendship.

My other humorous book, *The Unflushables* is a pictorial review of antique outhouses from decades ago. It documents a slice of history that no longer exists. It pictures more than a hundred historical outhouses including two, three and five story unflushables along with those of presidents and unusual situations.

The memory of a smile lasts forever

From **Missouri** The *Show Me* State

"Inflation is what we pay for free government benefits."

A good life would be impossible without humor

From
Washington
The *Evergreen* State

"America is where anyone can become president. To become a Supreme Court Justice is not so easy."

From
Indiana
The *Hoosier* State

"The way of the transgressor may be hard but it sure isn't lonely."

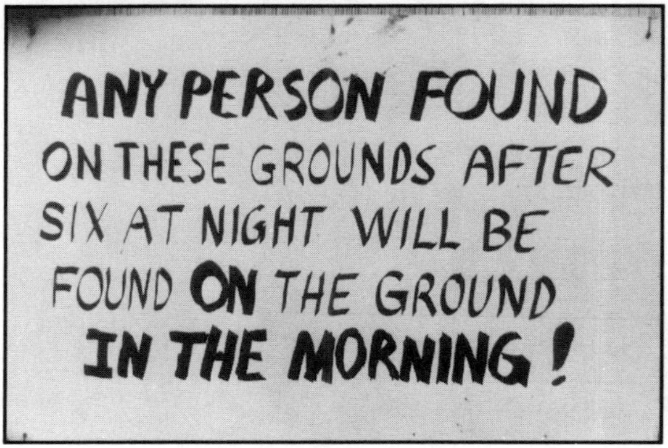

From
Saskatchewan, Canada

"They said to work hard, you will be rewarded- and I was with more work."

Good humor removes friction

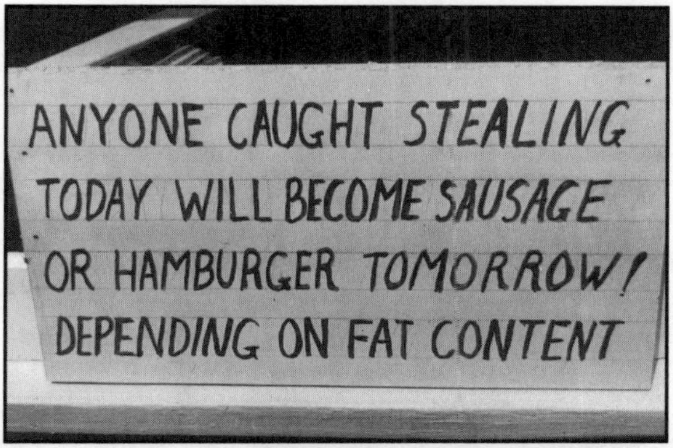

From
Kentucky
The *Blue Grass* State

"Most people go on a diet with the wrong equipment - a knife and fork."

From
Massachusetts
The *Bay* State

"I believe in living within my income even if I have to borrow to do it."

From
Montana
The *Treasure* State

"I don't want to start any arguments, I just want to explain why you are wrong."

A smile is nature's antidote for trouble

From
Pennsylvania
The *Keystone* State

"Grocery bags are stronger now. They used to burst with $10 worth of groceries. Now they easily hold $40 worth."

From
South Carolina
The *Palmetto* State

"I admire a good loser-as long as it isn't me. I just take one day at a time, that's all I can afford."

From
Indiana
The *Hoosier* State

"Money isn't everything, but it sure comes in handy when you lose your credit card."

I t took Noah 40 days and 40 nights to find a parking space

From
Iowa
The *Hawkeye*
State

"It isn't easy to get a parking ticket- first you have to find a parking space.'

From
Colorado
The *Centennial*
State

"One advantage of a small car is that you can squeeze twice as many into a traffic jam."

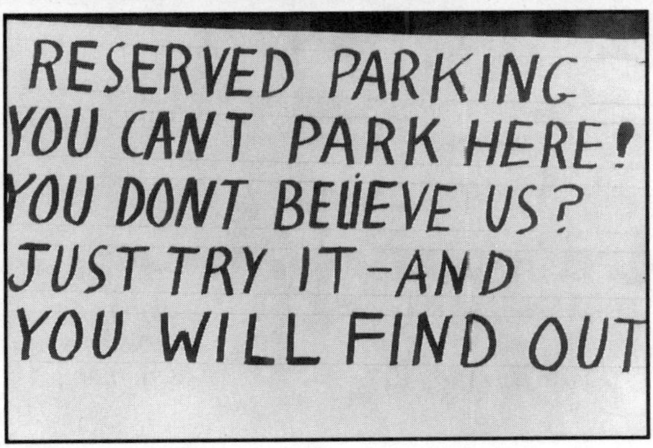

From
Montana
The *Treasure*
State

"Watch out for children, especially if they are driving cars."

Man's best friend

From
Alabama
The *Cotton*
State

"Dogs are dumb animals, but look who works so hard to feed them."

From
Illinois
The *Prairie*
State

"Do you know why the fastest dogs in the world live in Siberia? Because the trees are so far apart."
- Ira Hayes

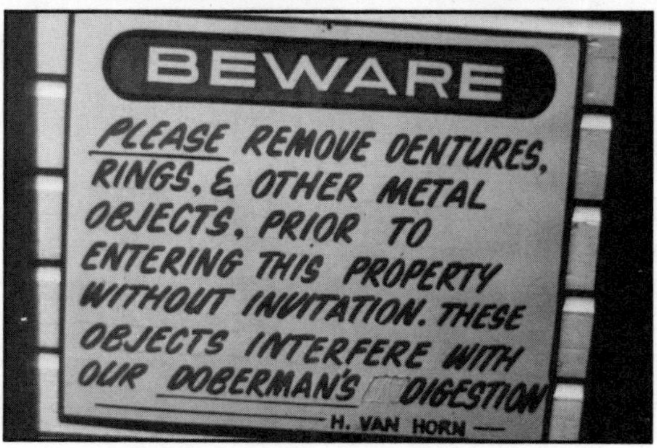

From
New York
The *Empire*
State

"Beware of the dog. He makes snap judgements."

Humor will fill your life with happiness

From
Wyoming
The *Equality*
State

"An added joy of giving instead of receiving is that you don't have to write thank you notes."

From
Texas
The *Lone Star*
State

"It is easy to spot a well-informed man today. He is totally confused."

From
Texas
The *Lone Star*
State

"Some people look for things to worry about. I met a man who wondered if the Declaration of Independence was notarized."

It's time to diet when your chin moves and the other one seconds the motion.

From
Florida
The *Peninsula* State

""I have been on a diet for 4 months and the only thing that gets thin is my hair."

From
North Carolina
The *Tarheel* State

"If God had really meant for me to be thin, he never would have given me a skin that stretches."

From
Maryland
The *Old Line* State

"I am a little depressed today. I looked at my birth certificate and found that I gained 179 pounds."

Humor shows people are well adjusted

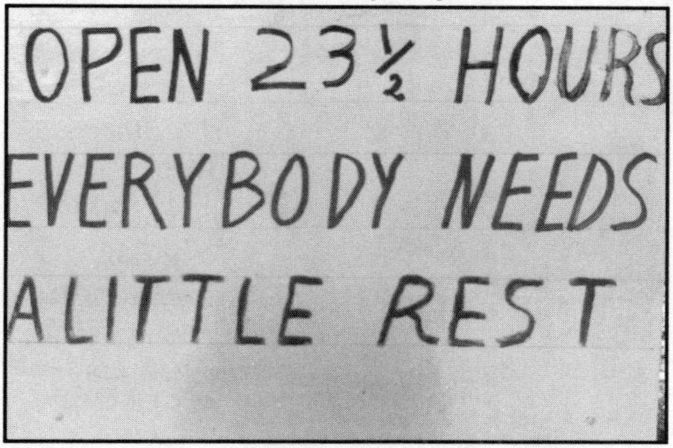

From
Mississippi
The *Magnolia* State

"Happiness would be a government that lived within its income and without mine."

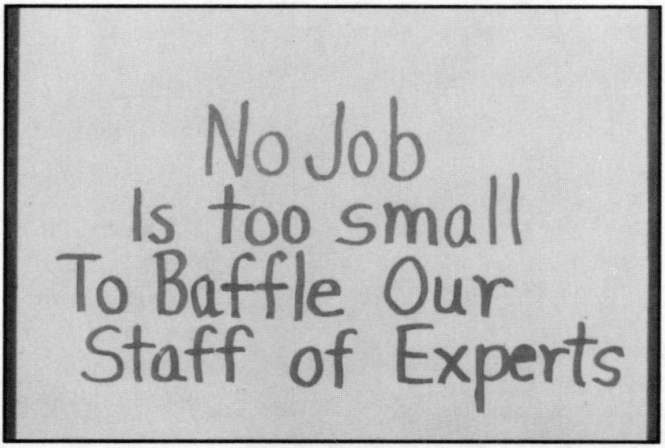

From
Indiana
The *Hoosier* State

"America is the only country in the world where a person is presumed innocent until the president offers him a job."

From
Oklahoma
The *Sooner* State

"A wonderful thing about money, it goes with any outfit you wear."

Money can't buy everything, take poverty for example

From
Georgia
The *Empire*
State
of the south

"An antique is something you can't use that can't be fixed at a price you can't afford."

From
Florida
The *Peninsula*
State

"One antique store had a sign, '$5 extra if we have to listen to what your grandmother had.'"

From
Indiana
The *Hoosier*
State

"One antique store sign said, 'If we don't have it we will make it today and you can get it tomorrow.'"

Bob Hope said, "I discovered the secret to eternal life. I lie about my age."

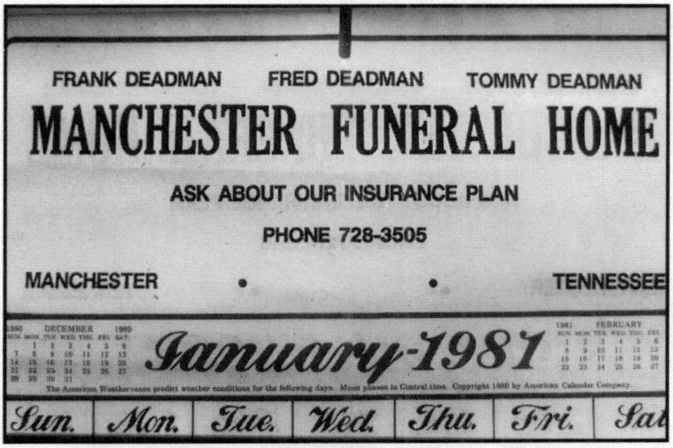

From
Tennessee
The *Big Bend*
State

"I'm so old my insurance company sent me a half a calendar."

From
Illinois
The *Prairie*
State

"You are getting old when you look at the menu before you look at the waitress."

From
Connecticut
The *Land of Steady Habits*
State

"The Bible says we bring nothing into this world and we take nothing out—so does the I.R.S."

Laughter is contagious

From
Pennsylvania
The *Keystone*
State

"The campaign promises of today are the taxes of tomorrow. Life just isn't fair. Earnings are minus tax and bills are plus tax."

From
Indiana
The *Hoosier*
State

"It has been reported that the average person spends eight months of one's life opening junk mail. Now it costs $1.25 to mail a letter. A quarter for a stamp and a dollar for a phone call to see if the letter got there."

No, you don't need an umbrella in a two story outhouse.

This two story outhouse was built in 1903 in Lundbreck, Alberta, Canada. It was connected to the second floor of a hotel. The outhouse survived when the hotel was destroyed by fire in 1963. It was moved to Heritage Park in Calgary in 1965.

The rear wall of the downstairs section of a two story outhouse is not the back of the building. The top deck seat is located all the way back, thus the offset walls form a chute down the back wall.

This is one of more than twenty two, three and five story outhouses in my book *The Unflushables.*

Thoughts on Health & Humor

"Now and then it's good to pause
in our pursuit of happiness and just be happy."
- Unknown

"Spring is wonderful.
It makes you feel young enough
to do all the things you're old enough
to know you can't."
- Franklin P. Jones

"May all your troubles last as long as
your New Year's resolutions."
- Joey Adams

Your Thoughts on Health & Humor

Zeph Telpner
Ervin Building, Suite 210
Post Office Box 1506
Council Bluffs, IA 51502
(712) 322-7763

Zeph Telpner

Zeph Telpner is a man with three careers, a speaker, a writer, and a certified public accountant. In 1966, Zeph fell asleep during a lecture on technical accounting and tax matters. That is when he decided that "all speeches must be yawn proof." He prepared his own technical seminars for CPAs, lawyers, and industry so that people could learn and laugh. This started his humorous speaking and writing career.

Zeph, the speaker, provides humorous or motivational after dinner and keynote speeches in addition to his seminars. He has been a member of the National Speakers Association for many years.

Zeph, the writer, is a featured columnist for two newspapers, in addition to his technical writing.

Zeph, the CPA, is considered an expert in taxes, accounting and litigation support by many law firms throughout the United States. He testifies as an expert in Federal and state courts. Yes, he still prepares income tax returns, too.

Zeph, a native of Iowa, is married and has four Children.

Humor Is Your Best Friend

By Zeph Telpner

"Without love and laughter there is no joy;
live amid love and laughter."

- Horace

Humor is people. When we think funny, perceive funny, and act funny, we are funny.

The late psychiatrist, Abraham A. Low taught that humor is our best friend. He said that everyday human experiences are filled with comic and trivial foolish thoughts, and events. He said that we can take what is said, thought, or done too seriously, and suffer, or we can see the humor in everyday life, laugh at it, and feel better.

My stories that follow come from the humor of everyday life.

Business

I'm a certified public accountant. No one thinks we're funny except a few clients when they receive my bill. Then they may ask if I'm trying to be funny. This hurts because I represent my clients only to the extent of their funds.

Many CPAs and taxpayers paraphrase Ben Franklin's quote that the only certain events are death and taxes. Death at least, is preferable to taxes. Death doesn't get worse each time Congress is in session.

Income taxes are easy. Placing a business phone call can be torture. Some employers and receptionists put self above customer. Recently, a telephone receptionist (TR) performed one of the funniest routines that I have ever heard. She or her boss probably hadn't planned the comedy, but I laughed anyway.

TR: X Company.

Caller: Bill Jones, please.

TR: Who's calling?

Caller: Why do you want to know?

TR: Who's calling?

Caller: You mean I can't talk to Bill unless you know who I am?

TR: That's right.

Caller: Why don't you try, "may I tell him who's calling?" You might get a better response.

TR: Okay. May I tell him what this is about?

Caller: Certainly. I want to discuss transfers to controlled corporations in exchange for stock and securities under Code section 351 when the basis is determined under Code sections 354, 355, 356, and 357.

TR: Huh? What?

Caller: Why don't you just put Bill on the line.

TR: Who's calling?

Caller: Zeph Telpner

TR: Huh?

Caller: Zeph. It's spelled Z-E-P-H.

TR: Z-E-L-P-H?

Caller: No. There's no "L" in my name.

TR: What's Noel got to do with it?

Caller: It's Zeph. It rhymes with Jeff.

TR: Zelph?

Caller: No. Listen. It's easy. Z as in Zebra. E as in elephant. P as in parrot...

TR: Are you for real?

Caller: It's like Jeff with a "Z."

TR: Oh! Zeph! I've got it. What's your last name?

Caller: Are you kidding? How many Zephs could he know?

TR: Don't holler at me.

Caller: Who was I calling?

TR: Don't ask me.

Mothers

Mothers always have homespun wisdom from long years of raising children and keeping grandparents from completely taking over. My mother always had unwavering faith in God and in her children. For many years, though, I thought that her advice was naive. If I was afraid to ask a girl for a date, mother said, "don't worry. God will provide."

When I thought I would fail a test at school, mother said, "God will provide."

When I was sent overseas during the Korean War, I thought that I might not return. Mother said, "you'll come home. God will provide."

After my mother's death, I found that she was right. I started to lose my hair, but God provided. The faster my hair fell out of my head, the faster it grew out of my ears.

My secretary asked, "what's that toilet paper doing on your ear?"

"I cut myself shaving," I answered.

Exercise

CPAs, and many others, sit at desks for too many hours. They don't keep in shape. My doctor told me to get strenuous exercise so I took up judo.

My judo teacher, Vern, taught me to throw, strangle, twist joints, and to grapple with an opponent. Judo is Japanese for the "gentle way."

Vern was a great coach. In my first tournament, I won second place in the heavyweight division. While I awaited my match, my self-confidence waned. I was thirty-one. Most competitors were in their twenties.

"Don't worry," Vern said. "You won't win the tournament. You're inexperienced, but you'll at least take second place."

"Are you crazy?" I said. "My heart's in my mouth, and I'm scared."

"I'm telling you, you'll win second place."

"How can you be so sure?"

"There's only two heavyweights in this tournament," he said. "Get out on that mat. You'll win second place."

After a few years, I taught a self-defense class. Self-defense techniques must be made simple. There are, for example, only two simple steps to remember when defending yourself against a gun.

Step one: There is a hole in the end of the barrel.

Step two: Don't stand in front of that hole.

Dressing For Success

I wore stylish silk suspenders long before the suspender fad. Many people ask if I wear them to be in style. I nod wisely, and they believe that I always wear the latest in modern fashion. I don't really wear suspenders to be in fashion.

I wear suspenders because several years ago my son, Joel, took me shopping for suits in New York City where he lived. As I tried on several suits, I recalled that the necktie of a successful businessman must reach his belt or hang just below it. I was doomed. As I reached middle age, my stomach reached middle size. Each morning when I dressed, my tie reached to my belt or just below it. After an hour or two, my chest would descend to my stomach, push my pants down to my hips, and I would walk on my cuffs. This created a large gap between my tie and my belt. I had violated the necktie rule.

To correct this gap, whenever I bought a new suit, I'd wear the pants low on my hips to be fitted for alterations. Then, each morning I could pull my pants up so that my tie and belt would touch. When my stomach eventually forced my pants down to my hips, I wouldn't walk on the cuffs.

In New York, I casually pushed my pants down to my hips for my fitting. The tailor had immigrated from Italy. He had a thick Italian accent. Before he measured my inseam, he jerked my pants up high and said, "you gotta wear you pants uppa here."

I pushed them down. "No. If I wear them high, after you alter them, they'll slip to my hips. I'll walk on the cuffs."

"You gotta wear 'em here." He jerked them up again.

I pushed them down—he pulled them up. I pushed them down—he yanked harder to pull them up. I yelled at him with my new soprano voice. "Stop pulling my pants up."

"No! You gotta wear 'em here."

"They'll be too long."

He was exasperated. He shouted, "Then, you gonna wear suspenders." He sewed suspender buttons on my pants.

Why do I wear suspenders? I wear suspenders to avoid life as a soprano.

Health

Stop smoking. My kids said it. My wife. My brother. My friends. Everyone told me to stop. I was a four pack a day smoker, and a thousand cough a day cougher. Nothing could stop me. Nothing, that is, until I started to earn a living from speaking. I no longer could afford to die early from smoking. The pay for living was too good.

Finally, I stopped smoking. It was the easiest thing that I have ever done. I used muscle control. If I wouldn't let my hand muscles pick up a cigarette, I couldn't smoke. If I wouldn't let my arm muscles put a cigarette in my mouth, I couldn't smoke. If I refused to let my hand muscles light my cigarette, I couldn't smoke. And even if I lit the cigarette, and placed it in my mouth, if I wouldn't let my mouth muscles inhale, I couldn't smoke. It worked. After four packs of cigarettes a day, I quit.

But—I had an ulcer. When I stopped smoking, I became so nervous, that my ulcer got worse. I couldn't keep food down. I couldn't enjoy life. I was desperate. I was torn between smoking and not smoking. Between my stomach and my throat. I discovered what I thought was the best of both worlds—smokeless tobacco!

I chewed, constantly. Every waking hour, a wad of tobacco rested between my lip and my gum. Cowboys chewed it. Athletes chewed it. Chewing was socially acceptable. I was content. Then—my dentist warned me of oral cancer.

I felt secure, though. My dentist, and my otorhinolaryngologist examined my mouth, regularly.

As I chewed more and more tobacco, my voice became hoarse. While presenting a two-day seminar, my voice gave out at the end of the first day. A substitute instructor finished for me. "No talking for six weeks," my doctor had said, "or you may never speak again."

I decided to use my muscles to give up my beloved chewing tobacco. If my hand muscles wouldn't pick up the can, I couldn't chew. If my finger muscles wouldn't put the tobacco in my mouth, I couldn't chew. If my mouth muscles kept my mouth shut, I couldn't chew. I stopped cold turkey, but a strange sadness swept over me. I experienced a terrible surge of loneliness. I felt as if I had lost a dear friend. I relieved these feelings with chewing gum.

I was happy again as I chewed 18 or more sticks of

gum a day. I chewed and spoke, and chewed and spoke. I became hoarse, again. My throat was sore, and I had a continuous earache. I worried about my voice. "You have temperomandibular joint pain-disfunction syndrome," my doctor said. I gasped. I almost fell to the floor. I was worried.

"What's that?" I said. "And, is there something easier to call it?"

"You can call it TMJ."

"What does all of this mean?"

"It means that you chew too much gum. Don't chew anymore."

I was shattered. I had once thought there could be no life without cigarettes. Then, I had believed that there could be no life without chewing tobacco. How could there be life without my chewing gum as my security blanket? Everything was hazardous to my health.

What is the treatment for TMJ? One aspirin every six hours, and a soft diet. I can't take aspirin. It irritates my ulcer. A TMJ soft diet doesn't mean soft boiled eggs. A TMJ soft diet means you eat only food that can be eaten without teeth. You puree your meals in a blender. For two weeks, I ate mashed potatoes, and pureed tuna fish. If you ever have to drink a can of tuna, you will never, never, never chew gum again.

This diet increased the diameter of my waistline. Soft foods are often high calorie foods. Ice cream is soft. Avocados are soft. Pureed Spam is soft.

Growing older is also hazardous to my health. Without tobacco or gum, I feel older than I am. What must I give up next? My wife is worried.

Proverbs

Proverbs have long been offered to us as wisdom. A rolling stone gathers no moss is one that is accepted as a profound truth. But proverbs really come from the humor of everyday life. Anyone can create a proverb. It's easy. Take my latest one for example. "The farther from home, the better your memory."

I thought of this proverb on the way to work one morning. I drove fifteen miles to my office. As I got out of my car, I thought, "Woops. I forgot to unplug the coffee pot." When I left home, I hadn't even thought of the coffee pot. After fifteen miles on the road, my memory had improved.

Average alertness would have suggested to you, the proverb that "mass murderers are the best neighbors." During a recent interview, a neighbor said, "I can't believe that Joe shot 26 people. He was the nicest person. Always quiet and polite. He used to babysit with our kids. I'd trust him with anything I own."

The reporter asked, "how about your gun?"

"I don't think so," said the neighbor.

Children

Three of our four children were home from college for the summer. In the fall, our youngest child would join his brothers and sister to attend college. I recall that final September when all four left our nest. My wife and I stood in the yard to hug and kiss each one of them. As they drove away, we stood in silence to follow their automobiles with our eyes until they were out of sight.

We turned to one another. Our eyes were wet—our voices choked. I couldn't speak. What could I say? Then my wife spoke to return me to reality. "Do you realize," she said, "that for the first time in fifteen years, you'll have to mow the lawn, shovel the snow, and carry out the garbage?"

I couldn't hold my tears back.

Quarrels

If most of us could see the humor of trivial happenings, we wouldn't quarrel as much. Each day we hear of tragedy from trivialities.

A woman murdered her husband of thirty-five years. "He always left the toilet seat up. I've nearly fallen in each night for thirty-five years," she told the police, "so finally, I shot him." She could have lowered the seat herself, laughed and avoided a lengthy trial.

"My wife never put the cap back on the toothpaste tube, so I strangled her." a husband confessed. He could have replaced the cap himself, laughed and stayed clear of prison.

Somewhere, a husband and wife are reading the papers and watching television.

Wife: Johnny Carson is paid $12 million a year. Don't you think it's terrible that he gets paid so much?

Husband: He's worth every cent. He's funny, and he's on three nights a week—sometimes, more.

Wife: But most of us work much harder. We can hardly get by on what we earn.

Husband: Well, he's got talent and deserves to earn millions.

Wife: But he gets paid way too much. He doesn't work hard at all.

Husband: You think so? I'd like to see you make it to the top the way he did.

Wife: You never agree with me. You always have to be right.

Husband: And, you're always saying stupid things.

Wife: You're a stupid jerk.

Husband: You're a moron.

Neighbor: Well, they really got loud. Then they started to throw things around. I phoned the police when a dish flew through the window.

Police report: Four of us spent almost ten minutes pulling them apart. Bruce grabbed the husband. Then the wife went crazy and jumped on Bruce. She broke his glasses before we could pull her off. We suffered more injuries than they did.
Reporter: What were you fighting about?
Husband and wife: Johnny Carson's salary.

Jobs

When I was fourteen, I took a job as bus boy at the local hotel. My first day didn't go the way I wanted. I helped with a luncheon banquet. I set tables and carried food trays to the serving stations of my assigned waitress.

I had never been to an elegant banquet. Community leaders filled the tables. The chefs had worked overtime. The chicken was luscious, and a beautiful golden brown. Large and bright green peas flanked the chicken on its right. On its left, creamy white mashed potatoes molded themselves against the chicken. Orange carrots and spiced apples completed the plate.

A lone man walked in. He was late. Everyone else had been served. The waitress was swamped. She told me to pour him a cup of coffee.

I was thrilled. He was the principal of my junior

high school and had once asked me to be the emcee at the school assembly. "Hi," I said. I wanted to be cool. Not just because he was my principal. I had a crush on his daughter.

I didn't know that you should pour close to the cup. I held the pot at shoulder height, aimed it at his cup, and let the steaming hot liquid begin its rapid descent. That coffee defied the law of gravity. I watched in horror as it splashed hard into his cup, hit bottom and started up the other side—and onto my principal.

When he yelled at me, his voice was several octaves higher. I ran off, yelling for the waitress. She dried him with a soft white towel while I hid in the kitchen. In my mind, future emcee opportunities had disappeared, and my love life was ruined.

I took my lunch break. The help ate chop suey that day. Just as the chef slapped a ladle of hot and pale looking chop suey onto my plate, the waitress hollered for me to bring a meal to my principal. I thought that my plate was for him.

This was a chance for me to redeem myself. I hurried into the dining room, served the chop suey to him, apologized for the coffee, and retreated to the back wall. He stared at his chop suey and slowly turned his head to see what others were eating. He looked at the other chicken dinners and stared again, at his chop suey.

When I saw him motion for the waitress, I ran for the kitchen. I removed my white jacket and quit my job. I didn't ask the principal's daughter for a date. I had discovered that chop suey does not promote romance.

Humor is Your Best Friend

Laughter makes us feel better. When we can see the humor of everyday trivialities, we will realize that life is worth living. Someone once said, "laugh and the world laughs with you. Eat onions, and you cry alone."

Don't cry alone. Laugh with the world.

Psychiatrist Dr. William Fry
of Stanford University suggests,
*"Look for the humor in an angry situation.
Search for it. If you are standing on the street
and someone drives by and splashes gutter water on you,
you might yell and shake your fist.
Or you can take another look, see the humor, and laugh.
The stress and anger will disappear.*

Thoughts on Health & Humor

"There's nothing worth the wear of winnning
But laughter and the love of friends.
- Hilaire Belloc

"Joking and humor are pleasant,
and often of extreme utility."
- Cicero

"And more then wisdom, more than wealth,
A merry heart that laughs at care."
-Henry Hart Milman

Your Thoughts on Health & Humor

Jim McJunkin
McJunkin/Odum
327 W. Bancroft
Azusa, CA 91702
(818) 334-2312

Jim McJunkin

Jim McJunkin has been speaking professionally since 1979. He has given hundreds of speeches and seminars throughout the United States. He is an award-winning Toastmaster, and belongs to the National Speakers Association. Some of the positions he has held that have given him this "hands-on" experience are: Director of Marketing and Sales, Swintec Corporation; Vice President of Marketing, Micronet; Assistant to the President, Scientific Data Systems; Sales Manager, Lanier Company; Sales Manager, Pitney Bowes; Operations Manager, Bank of America.

McJunkin/Odum & Associates trains salespeople and managers, conducts dynamic seminars, and provides consulting services to numerous businesses in the continental United States. Some of the organizations they have addressed are: Xerox, Avery International, Pitney Bowes, Lanier, Ameron, Century 21, Swintec, Peppardine University, and Pacific Bell. It is their belief that attendees want a volume of nuts-and-bolts information, and that this information is best assimilated in a humorous, entertaining, interactive atmosphere.

Selling, Smiling & Serving

By Jim McJunkin

"Choose a job you love
and you will never have to work
a day in your life."

- Confucius

A sales career gives me the opportunity to serve my customers, help them, and make them smile. I love the business because it allows me to live my philosophy. Selling is not only the oldest and greatest profession in the world but the sales profession has more humor than any other profession. Pulling someone's tooth, snipping out an appendix, or making out tax forms are not hilarious. But being a sales professional and sales trainer has kept me and my customers laughing for over twenty years.

Selling is like acting. Salespeople are only as good as their last month's record. The sales profession is easy to enter—and easy to leave. Lots of people begin selling that perhaps should have considered another profession, or continued with their old one. Tommy Tepers was one of these. Tommy and I were hired together as beginning salespeople at an office equipment company.

Tommy was a very good looking man. Very impressive. He was six foot five, with thick jet black hair (I always accused him of dying it), slender and athletic. Since I am bald (hair is useless and costly), I especially noticed that abundant head of hair. He had a voice that you imagined was like Abraham Lincoln's.

He possessed the great skill of memorizing the company sales script perfectly. I, however, always kept wanting to ask the customers what they needed and wanted. So I tended to wander away from the set script the company insisted on.

Our sales manager required us to recite this company script in a presentation to another salesperson, in front of the class. Tommy was easily the star of the group. His rendition was like a copy machine copy of their script. I wondered how I could keep my heart in it when I love people so much. I like to look in their eyes and listen to what they say. A set script is difficult for me. I realized my natural instincts were not company policy. Tommy was the man they were looking for. I felt like the last kid to be chosen for the baseball team in 3rd grade.

Then on the second day of our training, it was time for freelance role playing on camera. There were fifteen of us novice salespeople. I was number eleven, Tommy was number twelve in the lineup.

Movie star handsome Tommy seemed uncommunicative and almost sullen that day. He sat at his desk with his back straight, both legs on the floor, his hands folded on the desk. His eyes were half closed and glazed over. I noticed he did not look up once. The closer the presentation got to us two, the greener his face got.

I was stumbling along with my presentation when the attention of the whole class became riveted on Tommy. I hoped it was not my performance that affected him. He stood up, grasped his mouth with both of his hands and staggered out of the sales class, thus missing his place in line to perform. He didn't leave his room for two days, telling his boss over the telephone that he had caught the flu.

I believed his story until I had the great experience of riding with him on his sales calls one day. We were assigned as partners, and given a territory to explore for new customers. This activity is called "cold call." It seperates the men from the boys in sales, as knocking on doors of people you do not know is the number one fear of salespeople. Tommy wanted me to do the cold calling in the morning. I was agreeable to lead off. I always love to find new customers, and especially enjoy learning about their problems so that

I can help them. I wake up every morning with the belief something wonderful is going to happen to me before noon. If it doesn't happen, then I make it happen. The way I feel about cold calling reminds me of the line from Shakespeare that says, "The sun will not be up as soon as I to greet the fair adventure of tomorrow!"

It was a great morning. We found many new prospects who needed office equipment. I met several new friends to help during the morning.

I was glad something wonderful happened in the a.m. because nothing good happened in the p.m., especially for Tommy. After lunch I thought, "Now, since Tommy is so great looking, and uses the company script perfectly, our two-man team will win the sales contest at the end of the day!" I had waited many weeks to see handsome Tommy in action, and couldn't wait to hear his beautiful voice, strong presence, and perfectly memorized sales talk. I figured he had to be an awesome force in action with prospects. Instead I learned a great lesson.

Tommy did o.k. in front of the prospect, that is, he seemed all right until it came time for him to talk. To this day I've never seen a man perspire like that. When the prospect asked Tommy questions, his answers were in English words, but not in English sentences. He mumbled in bits and pieces without a smile anywhere.

I was totally confused because I knew what Tommy was supposed to be saying. Finally the prospect dismissed us, saying he was busy and could not waste any more time. The interview must have been five minutes but it seemed like an eternity because my heart was bleeding for Tommy. We never learned what the prospect's needs were so that we could make a proposal. As we walked out of the office I looked at Tommy with great sympathy, realizing he had been paralyzed with fear.

I will never forget the words he said to me. "I should close that one tomorrow." Then he explained to me what a great job he had done.

Tommy taught me that you can learn all the perceived skills of a salesperson but unless you have three elements, you will not succeed in the profession of selling and serving customers. The three things Tommy lacked were:

1. Caring more about the customers' needs than about his own. Tommy was concentrating on himself, not on the customer.

2. Possessing enough **Self-Esteem** so that he could take his work seriously, but not himself.

3. Courage to rise to each day's challenge and succeed no matter what frustations and rejections occur, because of an inner conviction that there is always someone who needs us waiting around the corner for our service and our smile.

Tommy taught me that what can be seen on the outside of a human being is not nearly as important as the love of helping people that dwells within their heart. That warm, shining, humorous spirit is the factor that makes the difference. Clothes, hair, height, memorizing scripts, knowledge of products are important, of course, but unless the salesperson puts the interests of the customer first, none of the other things count.

Hidden from the Nazis, Ann Frank wrote in her famous diary, "Whoever is happy will make others happy too. If you have courage and faith, you will never perish in misery." That day with Tommy I decided to give every human being I meet the gift of joy, help, and personal interest. I have found this method turns prospects into customers, and customers into lifelong friends. Dottie Walters said of me recently, "We always love to see you coming, Jim, because you not only help us with our business needs, but you light up our day with your smile." She didn't mention my clothes, hair, or height.

Are Great Sales People Born Happy?

Many times I've heard people say someone was "a born salesperson." Oh, how that statement makes me cringe. People used to tell me all of the time, "Jim, you are a natural salesperson. You ought to get into sales." I seemed to be trying to prove that theory wrong in my first two years in sales. I bombed. If you have an outgoing personality and are a little funny, it does not mean you will be a great salesperson. (but it helps!)

Sales can be a painful experience if you don't prepare yourself for it. Rejection is the hardest thing to cope with. Some prospects treat salespeople as if they were going to steal their first-born. Every company, every business, every government on this earth depends on sales. This book you are holding in your hand is a good example. Someone sold the lumber to the mills. The mills sold the paper to the printers. The printers sold the books to the publisher, and on it goes until the product finally reaches the hand of the end user. In all of the everyday things we take for granted there are hundreds of salespeople involved. When free enterprise is at work we have a myrid of choices. The opposite of the free enterprise sales system is communism, where the government does all of the selling. The result of that system is little merchandise in the stores and long lines waiting to buy that small selection.

Today, the great changes and opening of the doors of trade in Russia and China testify to the fact that free enterprise works. Even at the heights of government, we find diplomats who sell concepts to the other countries of the world. The truth is as the great sales personality and Chairman of the Board of *Parade Magazine,* Red Motley, said, "Nothing happens until somebody sells something."

It Helps to Be a Little Crazy

To be successful in sales, you must find a wonderful product to sell. It must be one that you believe in with all of your heart. Then you must want other people to have the benefits of your product. I tell my sales seminar attendees that it helps to be a little crazy. By that I mean you must have a delicious sense of humor. If you take your work too seriously, you set yourself up for a very stressful life. I love the Harry S.Truman quote, "If you can't convince them, confuse them!"

Which brings me to a story: In my younger days (why do people say "younger days" when we tell about ourselves? Maybe it is to contrast with our "wiser days.") I worked for a very good company selling computerized billing services to the medical profession.

No one on this earth understands rejection better than a salesperson who makes a living selling anything to medical doctors. Doctors are great people who are trained to help sick people and save lives. They are not trained to make business decisions. For that reason, they tend to treat salespeople like a disease! My first six weeks of trying to serve the doctors' needs was pure hell. They didn't like me. Could it be because I looked too healthy? I kept seeing sick people coming in and wondered which one of them would give me their illness.

No one would talk to me. Of course I loved waiting for hours in doctors' offices at first, because I got to read all of the ancient magazines I had missed in the last five years. But even that grew less exciting after the eighth or ninth time around. I became bored and frustrated.

Doctors whom I had been waiting to see for three hours would walk past me on the way out. They'd just look at me long enough to see that I appeared well. Then they ignored me and strode right out the door for whatever emergency called them. I suspected it might be golf.

The day I realized that the medical sales field was not for me (or you could say I was fired—multiple choice) I had finally found a person who would listen to me! It was an office manager in the small desert town of Hemet which was about 125 miles from my office. I was working the desert area that week to punish myself for leaving a great sales job to come to this one. It was about 145 degrees in the shade, about 2:30 on a Thursday afternoon. When the woman said she would be happy to talk with me I panicked—no one had said that to me in six weeks!

I took the macho way out, and told her I was new. I asked if I could come back tomorrow with my sales manager and make our professional presentation.

When I explained my first hot prospect to my boss, Ron Castlepress, he was not extremely happy at the prospect of that long, hot drive. I told him I needed him. He could see I was on my last legs on the job and figured this first sale might revive me, and get me going.

So Ron and I drove out to Hemet the next morning. At eleven a.m. it was 101 degrees. The car overheated. We turned off the air conditioner in order to keep the car running, and proceeded to melt into puddles of perspiration. I told Ron not to worry. This was a great opportunity to show our mettle by overcoming obstacles to success. At that point he grimly asked me if I had ever undergone therapy.

When we arrived, we had sweated through our shirts. Rivers ran down our backs. But we resolutely kept our warm suit coats on in order to make our dynamic business impression. I just knew it was going to be a great day when the office manager, who was a little rotund, asked how far our office was from Hemet. I told her it was about 125 miles. She asked if we had run the whole way. I exploded with laughter, but when I noticed Ron did not crack a smile, a chill entered my heart. I should have picked up the warning signs then.

Ron started the presentation with me flipping the big flip chart that explained our medical billing system whenever he gave me a secret command. Things were going real cool. The office was air conditioned. The office manager showed great interest and I was sure we would close the sale. Then Ron dropped the bomb. He asked her when the baby was due.

The office manager said quite bluntly, "What baby?" I of course exploded with nervous laughter, until I noticed neither of them smiled. She rose, walked to the door, opened it and told us to leave immediately. We folded up our materials and did so, with no words spoken.

I sensed that Ron was not a happy puppy after that call. So I said, "Let's go cold calling, and find another prospect. Ron said no. He wanted to get back to the office immediately. On the way home, Ron did not speak more than ten words all that long hot way.

It was certainly a rough ride with the temperature

soaring higher, and the air conditioner still not working. I tried to keep the conversation light. I laughingly told Ron not to feel too bad, as I had often made mistakes myself. I learned a lot from Ron Castlepress that day. He showed me a magnificent truth that seems to me a law as important as Newton's theory of gravity, or Einstein's law of relativity. I learned that sales managers cannot take a joke.

The last words Ron said to me that day, or for that matter, the last words he ever spoke to me were, "Turn in your car and stock immediately."

The moral to this story is never ask a prospect of either sex when they are due, and never try to tell jokes to your sales manager. So I left medical sales, because I found both the doctors and medical sales managers are dead (excuse the expression) serious.

Winners and Losers

Most people who do not make it in any kind of sales do not fail because they cannot sell their customers what they need. They fail because they cannot handle ups and downs. They think life and business are like a broad highway, and that all they have to do is keep the metal to the floor. Instead there are mountain roads and floods, and detours and blown tires.

Salespeople are sensitive. A salesperson can be a great success for twenty years, but when a bad month arrives they still ask themselves, "Am I a failure?"

Successful people in any field know it is the norm to have three great months a year, six good months, and three poor months and still be a magnificent professional. They look at the big picture. The same is true in science, discovery, and all kinds of business. Winners hang on through the tough times and figure out ways around detours. They are focused on the ultimate destination, not on the temporary setback.

When a salesperson has a bad month it usually affects their personal life. Sometimes the salesperson has no control over the reason sales are down. For instance, if they sell tax shelters and the government passes a new law that takes away the tax credit, the business is over. Bam. All gone. Sometimes it is timing—being in the right place at the right time. But most of the time when sales are down, the professional takes the responsibility (which they say is a sign of maturity).

I had an experience with timing to share with you. I was working for an office equipment company. My sales manager at that time was Jim Moon. Jim was, and still is to this day, the funniest man I have ever met, which made him the exception to the rule about unfunny managers. We were searching for new prospects together—cold calling. We called at car washes, gas stations and comic book stores. No business was overlooked. We walked in, and I would say we were both named Jim, and we sold stuff. Mr. Moon was not happy with my results. He motivated me by embarrassment, and played to my ego.

We finally found a man who would listen to our presentation. I told the prospect that our company could save him time and money. Mr. Moon very loudly told my prospect that we could NOT save him any time. I looked at Mr. Moon and said,"You can't talk to my customers like that! Our machines do save time!"

Mr. Moon ignored me, looked right at my prospect and repeated, "We don't save time. We only save money!"

I jumped out of my chair and got right into Mr. Moon's face, nose to nose. I yelled that I was going to tell our branch manager on him, and that he was as good as gone from our company. By this time, Mr. Moon had forgotten the man we were giving the presentation to. He grimly told me not to worry because the last act he would perform as a sales manager was to fire me.

I hotly replied that he could fire me all he wanted, but I would tell the branch manager about the contacts I signed for him that his customers had forgotten to sign on my first day on the job! Mr. Moon suddenly remembered our prospect, grabbed hold of himself, excused himself and left the establishment.

When I got back to the our office later that afternoon, Mr. Moon and the branch manager were waiting for me. As I walked down the long hallway, both of them stood at the far end. Their arms were folded. They frowned at me. My whole life flashed in front of me. This was the end of my sales career in office equipment.

Without saying a word they motioned for me to

come inside, to close the door behind us, and sit down. For the longest time, there was total silence. Finally, after what seemed like about two days, but was actually thirty seconds, the branch manager whose name was George Lumburg asked me what had happened that day.

I knew that my next words would set the stage for the rest of this exit interview. So I asked innocently, "What time of day are you talking about, Mr. Lumburg?"

Mr. Lumburg jumped up like a rocket. He pointed his finger at me, every blood vessel in his forehead sticking out over a quarter of an inch. He screamed as he told me that he had never heard of a salesperson who would argue with his sales manager in front of a prospective customer. Such a scene was the kiss of death to any chance that the prospect could become a steady client. Anybody in sales knew that. The prospect would never buy our products, or speak to us again. Our entire business image was hurt because of my actions in contradicting my sales manager.

Mr. Lumburg said that people like me were not welcome at his company. He told me to turn in my gear—words I had heard many times before. This would make the twelfth time I had been fired. I had been let go because a sales manager could not take a joke more than once.

But the kicker was, as I started to walk out of his office, I laid a large contract on his desk. It was with the same prospect who had witnessed our "time saving" argument. That was the most fun I ever had while being fired. By the way, they hired me back the next day. Mr. Lumburg and Mr. Moon still tell the story. But, of course, they don't let reality as I see it stand in the way of a good tale!

You might be interested to know, after Mr. Moon had left the office, the man we were talking to told me to sit down. He said how he used to be in sales and how his sales manager didn't know up from down. His great gift to me was, "Now what are you going to be selling me?"

Hung Up On Humor

Over the years I really was fired twelve times. Never for lack of production. Usually it was because the sales manager couldn't take a joke. I should have listened to my father when he told me, "Before you have an argument with your boss, take a good look at both sides. The boss' side and the outside."

I believe that the reason that many sales managers cannot take a joke is that they are in over their heads. They are the Peter Principal personified. Often they are those who could not sell. Someone upstairs in the company felt sorry for them and put them in a job where they just shuffle forms, and don't hurt anything. So they become walking "Murphy's Laws." I believe that the reasons people become sales managers are that they have no real skills—so it is the only job left to them. No wonder they can't take a joke.

So if selling is tough, although it may be the highest paid work in the world, why do millions of people enjoy being professional salespeople? Is it because people actually like abuse? Is it because we like to be humilated by our sales managers? No. It is because sales are the best, most enjoyable jobs in town.

Talk About Having Fun!

Selling is the profession for people who enjoy life and helping people with their problems. If you love laughing, and you can poke a little fun at yourself, you will be a champion in the sales field. Humor is a valuable tool that allows salespeople to deal with stress in a very positive manner.

Sales can be stressful. Deliveries are delayed. The wrong merchandise is packed. When it arrives it does not work. A million things can go wrong. Customers want, no, demand, that what they have ordered do the job they need done. They are right to do so. Things that go wrong might be the fault of your company, the weather, the economic situation, the time of the year, or maybe you did not ask the client enough questions so that you could recommend the correct equipment to solve the problem. If you allow the stess to build up like steam, it can blow off your head and your customer's as well. If you can get your customer to laugh while you hurry up and fix the mistake, you both win.

Really Difficult Customers

Some customers are harder to deal with than others. Doctors give the impression they don't consider salespeople human beings. They must have opened up a salesperson once and found nothing inside to fix.

I remember Dr. Tony Carce who had a practice in Azusa, California. Now, you may ask me why would a doctor have a practice in Azusa, if there even actually is such a place. Jack Benny put Azusa on the map when he broadcast on his famous radio show that he lived in California, a state with three cities named Anahieim, Azusa, and Cucamonga! He made people all over the globe laugh at those names.

I can't speak for the other two cities, but I can speak for Azusa. It is the only town in the world that ever had a MacDonalds close their doors and go out of business. The city is quite proud of that. But back to Dr. Tony Carce of Azusa. I made a sales call on Dr. Carce. It didn't take me long to discover he was a man who did not talk much. After an hour and a half of waiting in his lobby, I was finally put in his office to wait another 50 minutes. Medical sales often lead to deep meditation by sales people.

Finally Dr. Carce entered the room and sat down at his desk without a word. I introduced myself and made one-sided small talk. Things picked up a bit because he began grunting at me, which was an improvement over total silence. At least I thought so at the time. Right in the middle of one of the great presentations of my sales career, he suddenly swung around and faced the wall. All I could see was the back of the high leather executive desk chair.

I stopped talking. I waited. For five minutes there was total silence in the room. What could I do? Then all that meditating paid off. I came up with a way to handle this total rejection. I quietly got out of my chair without making a sound, tiptoed across the office and quietly opened the door. I slipped out and closed the door without making the slightest noise. I told the nurse that the doctor asked not to be bothered for an hour or more, smiled, thanked her, and left.

When I returned to my office my sales manager was waiting for me. To describe his mood is difficult. He was not exactly waiting happily. In fact no sales manager has ever waited for me happily. Anyway, he told me that Dr. Carce's office manager had called and complained that I had gotten up and left in the middle of my presentation.

"Sure," I told my sales manager. I explained that I had left because the doctor was dead. He had no body movement, no eye movement no visible pulse, and no response. That was my last day on that job.

Here was another sales manager who could not take a joke, I thought. It is a good thing that Dr. Carce was a doctor, because it might be difficult for him to handle being a sales manager. If there is such a thing as reincarnation, I hope I get to come back as the doctor and Dr. Carce becomes a medical equipment and systems salesperson.

Sales Are Profitable—and Fun

Eve must have enjoyed being in the produce business. There are those who say her apple was the first sale ever concluded. Some snake-in-the-grass manager put a bad light on the whole story. No sense of humor. Maybe that is why professions such as doctors, lawyers, dentists, CPAs and bankers have better press. If you ask ten kids under eighteen what they want to be when they grow up, few if any will say salesperson. Yet not one of these professions is successful unless it serves their clients' and patients' needs.

Pud, a young boy who is my neighbor, has been having troubles, so my son, Pud, and I talk together with him sometimes. Pud told us he was having a rough time deciding what he wanted to be when he grows up. He dismissed the medical and dental professions due to the yucky blood factor. I shook my head wisely. Me too! He decided that he didn't want to be a lawyer because lawyers fight with each other in public and on TV. And, of course, CPAs and bankers sit too much. I glanced at my back side and nodded agreement. I asked Pud had he ever thought of perhaps being a salesperson? After about 10 seconds of deep inner reflection, he looked up at me and just as seriously as one could expect, told me that he appreciated my concern for his future, but he wanted a "real" job.

Why is it that when we find a bargain on a car, or a home, or in buying a suit or even a business, we tell everyone we got a good deal...but when we pay more than we think is fair, we tell everyone the salesperson ripped us off? Maybe it is because we expect the salesperson to be on our side, and sometimes they are not. They play the adversary instead of the buyer's assistant.

So the next time a salesperson calls on you, tell them a joke and laugh at theirs. You may be surprised to learn how much they can help you find exactly what you need at a wonderful price, and you might find a friend in the bargain.

One last piece of advice to you as a buyer. The next time you are speaking with a salesperson, remember that sales make the free enterprise system go round and round. We all owe everything we own to the legions of hard-working, long-suffering salespeople.

Oh, one thing more. Never trust a salesperson with hair. As we all know, the brain needs lots of proteins. I contend that people with hair have had the protein sucked out of their brains. So they can't be honest. Look for a bald salesperson, male or female, and you'll enjoy a laugh, and a good deal.

"If you tell the truth,
you don't have to remember anything."
- Mark Twain.

Thoughts on Health & Humor

"Always leave them laughing
when you say good-bye."
- George M. Cohan

"Never let your head hang down. Never give up
and sit and grieve. Find another way.
And don't pray when it rains if you don't pray
when the sun shines."
- Satchel Paige

If you want to be not only successful, but
personally happy, then do your job
in a way that puts lights in people's faces.
Do that job in such a way that even
when you are out of sight, folks will always know
which way you went by the light left behind.
- Kenneth McFarland

Your Thoughts on Health & Humor

MEMBER NATIONAL SPEAKERS ASSOCIATION

Bill Wolff
1631 19th St.
Manhattan Beach, CA 90266
(213) 460-3356   (213) 546-1631

Bill Wolff

William "Bill" Wolff is an award-winning writer-producer for KNX-CBS NEWSRADIO in Los Angeles. He is the author of several best-selling non-fiction books dealing with human behavior, the dynamics of suggestion and applied metaphysics.

Most recently, Mr. Wolff has written and moderated a series of television programs featuring leading psychological and psychiatric authorities examining the cause, effect and treatment of agoraphobia, anxiety and executive "burn out."

An experienced and very popular seminar instructor, he and his wife, June, have led more than a hundred groups in the past two decades. Bill has taught at UCLA's Graduate School of Business and Management, various colleges and even a special class for inmates at a California-based federal prison.

He is an accomplished professional speaker and regularly addresses business, civic and professional groups on a variety of subjects. His favorite topics include Building Sound Self-Esteem, The Secret of Changing Destructive Stress to Success *and his most popular talk*, Laugh Your Way to Less Stress.

Whatever his subject matter, Bill Wolff always utilizes a generous helping of humor to emphasize his major points. Because of his comedic ability, he was booked as a stand-up comic at the Century City Playboy Club in Los Angeles. It was a unique experience for Bill to share the stage with country superstar, Kenny Rogers.

Laugh Your Way to Less Stress

By Bill Wolff

"The clown is brother to the sage."
- Arthur Koestler

The human community has invented some 3,000 different languages. You can be sure that whatever the language, it's rich with humor. Jokes, funny stories and satires seem to be common to all tongues. They serve a needed purpose.

Every culture seems to produce its share of clowns,

comedians and pranksters. I have no doubt that even in the most ancient of times, some fellow (I'm not being chauvinistic when I say it probably was a male, women being more sensible) stood on his head, took a pratfall or uttered some silly sounds to evoke a primitive laugh or two from his tribe on a stormy night as they sat around a blazing fire in some secluded cave eons and eons ago.

Of course, we'll never know who this first stand-up comic was but I can just envision him as he made the momentous discovery that it feels good, oh so good, in fact, heavenly, when your peers roar in glee at something you say or do. It was and is a "power trip."

You can be sure it wasn't the tribe's best hunter or bravest warrior. No, he probably was the guy who compensated for his lack of physical prowess by telling stories or maybe painting animals on the cave's wall.

With practice his skill at communication grew slowly but surely. He carved an important niche in his society. In medieval times every court boasted a jester. Poor indeed was the king who didn't employ some sly fellow able to earn his keep by prancing about all decked out in a colorful cap and bells. Interestingly, the jester was allowed to make comments and observations that few others dared utter in the presence of royalty. A liberating kind of lunacy characterized the professional fool's work.

Magical Art

It's a situation that still exists today. However, now (thank goodness) both men and women practice the almost-magical art of laugh-getting. It's my observation that some of the world's greatest clowns, stand-up comics and humorists are of the female gender.

As far as I'm concerned, you'll find the very best within the ranks of the prestigious National Speakers Association. One of my all-time funny people is surprisingly, not out of Hollywood or New York. She comes from the South (where seemingly emanate so many great speakers) and is an absolutely incredible performer.

Jeanne Swanner Robertson hails from North Carolina and bills herself as "the tall girl with the tall sense of humor." I wholeheartedly agree with her on both points. At 6'2" she is indeed tall. And anyone hearing her will immediately attest to the fact that she has a very tall sense of humor. Her power over an audience can be awesome.

Like so many genuinely funny people, Jeanne took what more than a few women would consider negative, and turned it into the centerpiece of her performance. That's the mark of a professional humorist. They poke fun at themselves and not at others.

The noted sales trainer and professional speaker Dave Yoho was born with a severe speech defect. Instead of capitulating to it, avoiding verbal communication, Dave Yoho was motivated by his congenital condition to rise above it and become one of the nation's leading speakers. He even pokes fun at how he once sounded. Humor is a vital part of all his presentations.

Timeless Wonder

Can anyone deny that people love to laugh? Laughter makes you feel good, and our basic need is to feel good. As author and comic Larry Wilde pointed out, "Laughter the timeless wonder drug, is the tension-breaker medicine that permits man to cope with the stark reality of everyday tragedy."

Wise would be the doctor who would have the insight to prescribe a solid session of laughter every morning upon rising. "Just listen to a cassette of Roy Hatten, Herb True or Charlie Jarvis," the medic could advise. "Before going to sleep be sure to read at least five pages of Robert Benchley, Mark Twain, H. Allen Smith or Woody Allen."

Laugh Break

There's plenty of scientific evidence strongly suggesting that laughter may very well contribute not only to alleviating illness but may act as a preventative as well. Question: How often do you make a conscious effort to take a laugh break?

Millions of Americans diet for good health; they engage in all manner of strenuous exercise regimes, spend time doing yoga, gulp down dozens of vitamins and yet the vast majority overlook what could be a most important contribution toward creating good health...namely, laughing on a daily basis.

Think about it. I'm sure that many people reading this book are avid runners. Some of you spend at least an hour a day running. Others can't wait to get on the golf course or maybe the tennis court. Yet, except for an occasional TV show or humorous movie (a rarity), few people really go out of their way to laugh. And yet this could be the key to maintaining continuing wellness.

Scientists are becoming aware that laughter is good medicine, primarily for relieving stress. They also suspect that it can cure headaches, fight infections and alleviate hypertension. So states a Newsweek report on science not too long ago.

Norman Cousins, the well known editor of the Saturday Review, practically became a folk hero of sorts among the holistic health crowd when he wrote in 1976 that he had laughed his way to health.

In 1964, Cousins became critically ill. He had just returned from Russia where he had served as the head of an American cultural exchange delegation. The diagnosis was (are you ready for this?) ankylosing spondylitis. In simple English, it was a degenerative disease of the connective tissues of the spine. The glue that bound his cells together was disintegrating.

He was so paralyzed he could hardly open his mouth. What's more the paralysis was spreading. Says Cousins, "I was told I'd have to make a choice between having my body freeze sitting up or lying down."

Hope springs eternal, goes the old cliche. And that was just about all Cousins had going for him. The doctors treating the noted intellectual offered him little in the way of encouragement. His chance for recovery, they informed him, was one in 500.

Cousins didn't buy that negative prognosis. In fact, he was certain that positive emotions like joy, hope, faith and the dynamic will to live could reverse his illness and actually banish the disease from his body. What he wanted was a permanent healing.

Hospital Stress

The first step, he reasoned, was to get out of the hospital, which he found to be a very stressful environment. With his personal doctor's permission (an obviously enlightened and rare medical expert) he checked out of the hospital and into a luxury hotel. He discovered that he was much more comfortable, the service was better and surprisingly, it cost a lot less.

On a borrowed movie projector from TV producer Alan Funt, he played some of the classic Candid Camera programs that never failed to make him laugh. He also acquired many of the Marx Brothers films that always broke him up no matter how many times he viewed them. His friends would read him funny stories, jokes and anything that could elicit a chuckle or two.

"I made a very interesting discovery," he says. "Ten minutes of solid belly laughing would give me two hours of pain-free sleep."

Cousins now lectures at a leading west coast university and has resumed his writing career. His book, *The Anatomy of an Illness*, is a must in anyone's library.

Quality of Laughter

Award-winning writer Susan Seliger, in the magazine *Self,* informed her readers about babies who are born deaf and blind, never seeing or hearing laughter, who nevertheless spontaneously smile and soon thereafter laugh, within weeks or months after birth.

By the time these infants are in nursery school, they begin to laugh when they accomplish a goal or anticipate such an accomplishment. As they get older, they smile and laugh more and more. Wouldn't you agree that laughter is a natural part of the human condition?

Patients at a gerontology center at the University of Southern California, it was reported, became more sociable and a lot more active when volunteers did funny, sometimes silly things aimed at reawakening the sense of humor lying dormant within the oldsters.

Help the elderly to laugh and you add years to their lives. That goes for all of us. Truth is, laughter not only increases longevity—it adds quality to the content of our existence. Isn't that what we all desire?

Great Joy

Every month I speak to a variety of business and civic groups as well as presenting SELF-ESTEEM/ STRESS MANAGEMENT seminars. I also appear on a number of radio and TV interview programs. It's obvious that I love to communicate and share ideas, information and workable techniques with people from all walks of life. However, my profession—in other words my bread and butter income—comes from my writing and producing efforts. And that too is work I dearly love.

I'm truly blessed because I enjoy the work I do. One of the most valuable parts of the seminar we present is specific (and I mean step-by-step information) on how to bring into your life that which will bring you great joy. Is it any wonder that I have a lot of fun?

At KNX-CBS NEWSRADIO I am associated with many interesting broadcast professionals. One of the wittiest is our traffic and weather reporter Bill Keene.

He is famous for using humor (in the form of outrageous puns) in his daily reports. It takes the curse off some piece of bad news such as a major freeway obstruction that means the listener is going to be late getting home or to work.

For instance: Keene reported that a ladder had fallen off a truck on the Santa Monica Freeway. He paused for an instant and then quipped, "Better be careful because the freeway is full of rung way drivers."

His job, he says, offers one of the few opportunities in broadcasting today for getting on the air and ad-libbing everything.

"It gives me a chance to let everything hang out. All the bad puns I've ever dreamed of crop up on Southern California freeways. They're just too good to let them lie there. You got to pick them up and use them."

And use them he does. If an opportunity presents itself, Keene will grab at it. Here's another example.

"A lot of dogs go over the fence because of the fireworks every Fourth of July. Right after one Fourth I heard this Highway Patrol unit on the eastside say: 'Hey, I got two dogs on the Pomona Freeway, it looks like a pack is following them.' And then I heard another unit say: 'There's at least six of them out there.'

"So I went on the air and reported that there was a sixpack of curs on the Pomona Freeway."

Definition of Humor

At the marvelous humor workshop during the 1982 National Speakers Convention in Chicago, Charlie Jarvis, truly a master at provoking laughter, sagely observed: "Humor is a painful thing told playfully." He also commented, "Humor is tragedy separated by time and space."

Some of Woody Allen's monologue jokes prove this poignant point. Divorce is obviously painful. And the diminutive Brooklyn-born mirth-maker has experienced it first-hand. Yet, he evokes gales of laughter from his sophisticated audiences when he uses the subject of his failed marriage as part of his stand-up routine.

"After six years of marriage, my wife and I pondered whether to take a vacation or get a divorce...and we decided that a trip to Bermuda is over in two weeks, but a divorce is something you always have."

When you start examining monologues, the name Johnny Carson immediately surfaces. Almost every adult video viewer is aware that Carson became a national institution when he succeeded Jack Paar as host of NBC's "Tonight" show.

He's a master at taking a joke and telling it in such a way that you almost believe it's a true story, something that actually happened to him.

"If I seem a little pooped I just got back from Indianapolis. And the flight was a little difficult. Just as I sat down a man came to me and said, 'Are you Johnny Carson?' I said, 'Yes.' He said, 'You know I was worried about this flight. I was really scared. But seeing you here...a man of your importance...gives me the confidence to take this flight.' Which wouldn't have bothered me, but he was the pilot."

Just as the laughter dies down, Carson tops the story with: "It kind of upsets you a little when you look into the flight cabin and the pilot has a St. Christopher statue on his dashboard and St. Christopher's got his hands over his eyes."

Zinger!

Early in this chapter I mentioned that the once male-dominated world of comedy has made space for the distaff side. The women have ably met the challenge facing anyone brave enough to stand before a group of strangers with the expressed object of making them laugh.

Ant that's exactly what a housewife and mother of five children decided she wanted to do more than anything else in life. There is no doubt that Phyllis Diller has accomplished her heart's desire and then some. Since her first engagement in a San Francisco night club in 1955, she has become one of the world's leading stand-up comics.

Her comedy trademark is the short, one-line zinger. She tells a lot of them in a little time. I've heard it said that Bob Hope goes for six huge boffs a minute. That's a pretty fast pace in anyone's league. According to some of Hope's writers who claim to have clocked Phyllis, she can get in a dozen quickies in just one minute.

Here's an example of Miss Diller's art:

"I've turned many a head in my day—and a few stomachs, too.

If I were a building—I'd be condemned.

When I got my first job I thought a filing system had something to do with fingernails.

My advice to brides: Burn the toast so he won't notice the coffee .

The year I finally lost my baby fat I got middle age spread.

Why is it when a couple has reached their fiftieth wedding anniversary, he looks like a little old lady and she looks like a little old man and neither of them knows the difference?"

According to my calculations that's just about thirty seconds worth of prime Phyllis Diller.

Humor School

For anyone interested in learning more about some of the biggest and established names in comedy, Larry Wilde (A talented funnyman in his own right) has authored a fascinating study on the subject, *The Great Comedians Talk About Comedy*. Serious students of humor might want to tackle Freud's *Jokes and Their Relation to the Unconscious;* Max Eastman's *Enjoyment of Laughter* or George Meredith's *An Essay On Comedy*. Steve Allen has also contributed to the field with a tome or two.

As for me, although I am an avid reader, I much prefer to drop by one of the fine comedy clubs springing up in most major cities and enjoy some of the brand new comics making their marks. The newer talents are willing to tackle most any subject as they go for the big laugh. For them, nothing is sweeter than the sound of an audience breaking up. Who was the philosopher that said, "Laughter is glory"?

Jimmy Alec, a deceivingly serious looking, thin and bespectacled young man in a nondescript suit, likes to poke fun at health food faddists, exercise and particularly those who run.

"Doctors say jogging is healthy for you. They claim if you run for thirty minutes you begin to feel light headed and euphoric. Know why? It's because you're so close to death. Ever see anyone who has run for over thirty minutes? (STARTS GASPING FOR BREATH) That does not look healthy to me.

You know who looks healthy to me? A person who has just eaten a pizza.

Why is it that junk food always sounds so delicious? I love those junk food names. Snickers, Chuckles and Twinkies.

On the other hand, health food has names like

Wheat Germ. If they want me to try that stuff they should have named it Wheat Ding Dongs. There are certain foods I will not eat just because of the name...Tongue. Did you know it was a cow's tongue? It never dawned on me that when I ate tongue it came from some poor cow. When I ordered Chocolate Mousse in a restaurant I didn't get some big hairy thing covered with hot fudge."

Laugh Process

Although I have appeared in a few night clubs, I do not consider myself to be a comedian, per se. However, I do employ a great deal of humor in all my presentations. I love to elicit laughter from those attending my talks. The truth is that I utilize a lot of funny material even in my seminars.

Dose of Joy

I have developed what I call a Laugh Process that I always schedule right after the lunch break during my one-day SELF ESTEEM/STRESS MANAGEMENT seminar. It has turned into one of the highlights of the program.

We present a lot of "meat and potatoes" type

material, important life-changing observable realities of human behavior. Somehow, a heaping helping of humor assists the seminar attendee to better assimilate the vital concepts that can transform their lives. I therefore utilize jokes, anecdotes and very special audio-visual tools aimed apecifically at this endeavor. Forgive me if I seem immodest but it works out beautifully.

In fact, I even incorporate a modified version (very shortened) in my one hour talk on *Changing Destructive Stress into Success.*

Self-Esteem is an emotion. It is how warm and loving you feel toward yourself. An important step toward getting my students to feel good about themselves is to "raise vibrations." One of the basic techniques is to get people to laugh and enjoy themselves.

Harvey Mindess, Ph.D., director of the psychology program at Antioch University, West in Los Angeles, insists that "One humorous remark can be as good as an hour's discussion if timed right and said right." I couldn't agree more.

Gag collector Joey Adams wrote: "Laughter is vaccine for the ills of the world. A dose of joy is a spiritual cure."

...ain't that the truth!

"Lay aside life-harming heaviness
And entertain a cheerful disposition."
- Shakespeare

Thoughts on Health & Humor

Dr. Fredrick Koenig, Social Psychologist
from Tulane University, explains,
"When you make yourself smile, you start feeling better. Concentrate on the humor of the situation. Take whatever is making you angry and give it a twist. Find the funny side. It works."

"A sense of humor is the pole that adds balance to our steps as we walk the tightrope of life."
- William A. Ward

*"Nothing is as funny as
something done in all seriousness."*
- Will Rogers

Your Thoughts on Health & Humor

Lilly Walters
Walters International Speakers Bureau
P.O. Box 1120
Glendora, CA 91740
(818) 335-8069

Lilly Walters

Lilly Walters is the Executive Director of Walters International Speakers Bureau. As a lecture booking agent she sends speakers, trainers and consultants all over the world. She gives seminars on how to hire speakers, program planning, and presentation skills.

Lilly is co-author of the book by Prentice-Hall, Simon & Schuster, Speak and Grow Rich - The Handbook for Professional Speakers; *author of the anthology,* The Great Communicators; *and a feature editor of the international magazine,* Convention World. *Her bureau is owned by her mother, famous professional speaker Dottie Walters, a pioneer of women on the speaking platform.*

Together, Lilly and Dottie publish the largest newsmagazine in the world for professional speakers, Sharing Ideas.

At the age of 12 Lilly began teaching horsemanship to the neighborhood children , organizing classes and holding mini horse shows. She obtained a Horsemaster degree when she was 18 and began a small training stable. She taught vaulting, the art of gymnastics on the back of a moving horse, and for 10 years her teams consistently brought home championships in regional and national competitions

They'll Hear You Better With Humor!

By Lilly Walters

"Eloquence is the art of saying things in such a way that those to whom we speak may listen to them with pleasure."
- Pascal

It's your turn to address your church, the local Kiwanis, or teach a training session at work. The presentation isn't for five months, so you don't have stage fright...right? Wrong! As Steve Allen says, "Stage fright is a deceptive term, it implies you will be frightened when you step 'on stage.' But in reality, you become frightened the minute you accept the assignment!"

So, how do you get the message home and keep from passing out on the platform? One sure-fire way is to hit your listeners' "funnybone." "But I'm not funny!" you cry in exasperation. *Au contraire*, let me give you a few ideas on how, when and why you can use humor to get your point across.

How To Motivate Your Listeners

Your communications will be judged by the response and changes they elicit in your listeners' actions and attitudes. There are five steps to motivate an audience. In every step, humor plays a vital role.

First: They must be ***listening.***
Second: They must ***understand*** what you are trying to say.
Third: They must ***believe*** you.
Fourth: They must ***retain*** what you say long enough to make a decision that will allow them to go on to step five...
Fifth: To ***act*** on the information you are imparting

Delivering a message to your listeners that they do not take action from is "like running your heart out in a relay race, passing the baton on to your teammate, who, instead of running with it, gives it to someone in the stands as a souvenir. If you as a speaker don't help your audience to remember your lessons, then you're wasting everyone's time." No message does anyone any good if it is just "left in the convention hotel with the towels (or most of the towels)," (from *How to Hold Your Audience with Humor,* by Gene Perret.)

How Does Humor Work In Communication?

Humor is largely graphic. We paint a picture with words, but the real message is an individual image that listeners paint in their minds while we are talking. The mind seems to remember graphics more readily than abstractions. A column of numbers is more difficult for the mind to fully absorb than is a pie chart or a bar graph. Then, comparisons done with images of houses, pictures of coins, etc. are even more easily ingrained into our memories (retained—Step 4) than the pie charts and bar graphs and therefore enable us to move into Step 5.

Danny Cox, a professional speaker, makes an excellent point with the use of humor on managerial effectiveness, especially procrastination. After delivering his serious point, he reinforces his message with humor. Danny says, "It's like we used to say back home…if you got a frog to swaller, don't look at it too long."

Danny uses the same process with another point about eliminating those people who won't subscribe to the team spirit, "We used to say on the farm that you can't teach a pig to sing. It wastes your time—and it irritates the hell out of the pig."

The graphic picture we paint in our minds when we hear these humorous anecdotes will be remembered long after we have forgetten the exact words of Danny's serious message. Yet, we will remember the point he is making.

Is My Message Too Serious for Humor?

"The more serious your subject, the more likely it may be unfairly categorized as pompous even before it's heard. It is your obligation to prevent the loss of your audience's attention and to restore balance and perspective. The best way to do that is with humor." (from *How to Hold Your Audience With Humor,* by Gene Perret.)

I was in an audience once for a presentation by a young lady who was an expert on dental hygiene. She came in dressed as the "tooth fairy" with a beautiful, flowing gown, a wand and lovely smile. Her press release said, "The woman who has been in more bedrooms than any other woman in the world!" Her audience was ready to laugh, learn and have a good time. Unfortunately, her smile turned into a serious expression and her slides went up onto the screen with pictures of pyorrhea. Never a joke, never a laugh. The audience started to slip out the back.

She asked me later, "What could I do to make them like me?" I told her, "They wanted to laugh. You had them before you started, but lost them because you didn't have an attitude of laughter and fun with them." She looked at me as if I was crazy. "Lilly, dental hygiene is a very serious subject, I want people to take serious action from my message, not laugh at it." She is out of business.

"A spoonful of sugar helps the medicine go down." (No matter how bad it is for your teeth, this kind of sugar will sweeten your listeners' attitudes toward you.

Humor Is An Attitude...What Is Yours?

Still think you're not funny? Many people think they are not really funny. Yet I sit with them at a dinner table or at a party and they make us all laugh. So why can't they do it on the platform?

We tend to take our inner mind's eye and focus it back on ourselves when we are giving a presentation. Our self-talk goes something like, "I hope they think I'm perfect." At a party, we are thinking about our friends and how we want to share the loving and laughing with them.

It's merely a change in our attitude when we step

in front of a group that closes off our natural funny and friendly self into the "phantom of the platform." Imagine the listeners in your audience are that same loving group of friends you let your hair down with.

Humor is not only jokes, stories, anecdotes, and such. It is also the attitude or spirit of fun, perspective, and balance that colors everything you say.

Most Common Mistake In Using Humor

The most common mistake speakers make when they use a humor story is not waiting for the laugh. A speaker's adrenaline flows at a much faster rate than the audiences'. You feel the audience has already had plenty of time to respond and they just didn't like the joke, so you rush on. As your experience grows, you'll know how long to pause.

Listen to your audiences' laughter on a tape after you speak. One person starts laughing, then another and another. Many people laugh because someone else did, not because anything you said was that entertaining. Give them time to digest the story you gave them, assimilate it, and then laugh.

Once you get them in a positive, happy, laughing frame of mind, they will start laughing when you raise an eyebrow.

Act Funny

Most novice speakers don't let their body in on the joke when they try to be funny. One of the greatest orators of all time was Winston Churchill. One of his tricks at getting a laugh is recalled by Hugh Walsingham: One always knew when it was coming. His own laughter began somewhere in the region of his feet. Then a leg would twitch; the bubble of mirth was slowly rising through the body. The stomach would swell; a shoulder heave. By this time, *the audience would also be convulsed, although it had no idea what the joke was going to be*. Meanwhile, the bubble had ascended a little further and had reached the face; the lips were as mobile and expressive as a baby's. The rich, stumbling voice would become even more hesitant. And finally there would be the explosion, the triumphant sentence of ridicule."

How Can You Be More Funny?

It is essential that you keep a diary, either on paper or on tape, of funny lines and stories you hear. Things that make **you** smile will have the best chance of making others smile when you repeat them.

What goes in, comes out. Feed funny things into your mind and funny things will come out of your mouth. Buy humor tapes, and watch comedy videos. Be careful of listening to too much off-color nightclub comedy. If you feed that in, it will come out at very inappropriate moments! There are literally hundreds of old Jack Benny, Will Rogers and George Burns tapes available now. All without a single off-color word, just good...no, outstanding humor! Pop one in every day. You will find your spirit uplifted and your natural dialog will become light and humorouImagine

"True humor springs not more from the head than from the heart; it is not contempt, its essence is love; It issues not in laughter, but in still smiles, which lie far deeper. It is a sort of inverse sublimity, exalting as it were, into our affections what is below us, while sublimely draws down into our affections what is above us," – Caryle, Essays: Richter

Humor Rules:

- Memorize the punch line
- Keep it short
- Rehearse it until it's second nature
- Don't blame the audience when it doesn't work
- Personalize your stories
- Laugh as you tell the joke
- Think funny.

Photo Credit: Steven Moeller, Irvine, CA

CURTAIN CALL

by Lilly Walters

We've shown you the challenge
Many skills to enhance.
It's all set before you.
Will you join in the dance?

You stride to the footlights
The crowd is so still.
Will they clap and applaud
And stand with the thrill?

Your words can bring courage
And hope and new powers,
For sombody crying,
In desperate hours.

The program is over
And gone is the crowd.
Did anyone hear you?
Did you come on too proud?

Did glitter and glamour
Cause you to forget
The caring and sharing,
Your mission neglect?

Reliving it later
Sadly parked in your car.
So much farther to go,
Yet, already so far.

Light knock on your door,
Says, "'fore you're off to bed,
Would you tell me more?
I just ***loved*** *what you said.*

Unsure of my part.
I was crying to day.
Your words touched my heart.
Do you mean what you say?

Were you talking to me?
I've a race to be run?
Is there power in me?
Did you mean...I'm the one?"

We've shown you the challenge
Will lives you enhance?
It's all set before you.
Will you join in the dance?

Thoughts on Health & Humor

"Mirth makes the banquet sweet."
- George Chapman

"But what avail the largest gifts of heaven,
When drooping health and spirits go amiss?
How tasteless then whatever can be given!
Health is the vital priciple of bliss."
- Thompson

"Laughing is the sensation of feeling good all over,
and showing it principally in one spot."
- Josh Billings

Your Thoughts on Health & Humor

Dottie Walters, C.S.P.
Royal Publishing, Inc.
18825 Hicrest Road
P.O. Box 1120
Glendora, CA 91740
(818) 335-8069

Dorothy M. Walters, C.S.P.

Dottie Walters is unique. She began her long and illustrious career with no car, one rickety stroller, two babies, a borrowed typewriter and a high school education. There were no jobs. The country was in a recession when Dottie started down the long road. She put cardboard in her shoes and kicked the wheel back on the stroller each time it came off.

Today Dottie is a World Class speaker, president of her International Speakers Bureau and publisher of the largest newsmagazine in the world of speakers, Sharing Ideas. *She has been honored three times by the National Speakers Association, with the Certified Speaking Professional designation, one of the first four United States women to receive it. She is a founding member of NSA, as well as the founding member of the Greater Los Angeles NSA Chapter. She founded the International Group of Agents and Bureaus and is Chairman of the Board of the American Association of Professional Consultants. She has initiated and sold several businesses, all based on advertising and publishing.*

She is currently president of four corporations, is an author, poet, speaker, seminar leader and publisher of anthologies featuring outstanding speakers. She has been featured in many TV and radio shows, newspaper and magazine articles, books and cassettes world wide. Her first book, Never Underestimate the Selling Power of a Woman *,is in its 15th edition.*

Most recently Dottie and her daughter Lilly Walters have written a book for Prentice Hall Inc., Simon & Schuster, titled, Speak & Grow Rich, *with a Foreword by Earl Nightingale.*

Dottie and Bob Walters have three children; one who is an attorney, another, a speech and communications teacher, and the third, the manager of Walters International Speakers Bureau.

Laughing, Loving and Learning

By Dottie Walters

*"If You Wait Upon Fortune,
You Can Never Be Sure of Your Dinner."*
- Benjamin Franklin

As a professional speaker and owner of an International Speakers Bureau, I am often asked by other speakers where to find good humor material. I believe the best is right in our own lives. If we can laugh at life, we bend a bit, instead of breaking. Whether we intend to use a funny, real life story in a speech, or as a stress breaker, we need to be on the lookout for material that will let people laugh. I find wonderful humor in great books, which are actually the repositories of the smiles of many lives. One of my favorites is the autobiography of Benjamin Franklin who holds up the mirror of life and shows us how to laugh at ourselves.

Funny Side Is Sunny Side

Often when my daughter Lilly and I work late at night on the graphics of our International Speaker's Magazine, ***Sharing Ideas,*** we get tired and short tempered. Then one of us will think of the silly side to a story we are placing in the magazine, and we start giggling. Suddenly we aren't tired or mad any more. You might like to try our idea when stress has you "up tight." Here is how to do it:

Take an ordinary circumstance and explore it to its ultimate conclusion. Example: While we were working on a story about a speaker who walked across America while writing beautiful poetry and appearing on radio and TV shows, we wondered about all the other people who walk, jog, step backwards, sideways, roller skate, bicycle, pogo-stick, & ice skate across the nation. We thought of dozens of new means of locomotion people could use to traverse the continent. By the time we got to the idea of ballet shoes, glass slippers, and hop-scotching across the country we were in gales of laughter.

Then we thought of the other side of the situation. What do the mayors, city fathers and mothers, and the ordinary people in the little towns along the way think of all this traffic on their main streets? Do they run out of keys to the city, or proclamations? Do they wake up each morning and ask each other, "Who do you suppose is coming today?" Do they take wagers as to the latest method of transportation? Eventually, do the townspeople slip out in the dead of night and turn the direction sign to their city the other way? We laughed until we almost fell off our chairs.

New Cure For Colds?

Every family has its oft-told funny stories that make wonderful material for speeches. My audiences love this one.

My mother was an advertising executive for the Alhambra Post Advocate. She tried many times to sell an ad to the fancy dress shop in town. Finally, Mr. Bragg said yes, and told her to come right over and pick up his material for the ad. She was ecstatic.

She dressed in her best clothes, and drove to the shop. Unfortunately she had a very bad cold in her nose, so just before she went in she felt down in the bottom of her large handbag and came up with an inhaler. She took off the lid and sniffed it deeply in each nostril. She said later that she noticed her nose felt better immediately. Then she marched into Bragg's, the most fashionable dress shop in town, smiling confidently. Everyone turned and gazed at her as she came in. She thought her outfit must be better looking than she had imagined.

When Mr. Bragg handed her the ad folder, he said nothing, but looked rather amazed, even shocked. Not wanting to give him time to change his mind, she clutched the treasured ad to her heart, and walked out briskly. She grinned as she noticed that her best dress once again turned every head in the shop .

She drove to the newspaper office, ran to her boss' desk, waved the ad folder at him and cried triumphantly, "I got it!" Her boss took one look at her and said,"What have you got? A strange disease?" He put his hands on her shoulders and turned her to look into the mirror on his office wall.

To her horror she saw that it was not an inhaler tube she had used so thoroughly on her nose. It was a particularly bright red shade of lipstick which gave her face a very unusual look.

Mom's lipstick saved my sanity a few years later when I finally landed an advertising sales appointment with a big department store in Palm Springs, California. In my car just before I went into the store, I mopped my face in the 120 degree heat, and pulled out my lipstick for a final dab. As I slanted the tube toward my mouth, the entire contents, which was liquid with the heat, poured over my white dress. I thought of Mom, laughed, and went right on in. The store manager laughed too, and signed the contract.

Later Mom married an outdoors kind of man who took her camping through Montana for their honeymoon. Mom had never seen an outhouse with two openings in the wide wooden seat. She sat down and absentmindedly set her purse next to her. Right into the aperture! Of course it had to be the handsomest Park Ranger in his impeccable uniform who brought the fishing pole to retrieve the purse for her while her groom looked on in fascination.

The Clock Struck Six Thirty?

I think true wild stories may run in the family. My beautiful redheaded daughter Lilly lost her front teeth in a terrible accident and wears a plate. At an exciting National Speakers Association meeting she had dinner at the "Western Night Party" held at a "Rustlers Roost"restaurant with a group of young speakers dressed in western garb. They all planned to learn to dance the Texas Two-Step after they put away steak and corn on the cob.

Lilly was to sing a duet on the NSA program the next day with Lee Robert, daughter of the Chairman Emeritus of the Association, Cavett Robert. Lilly smiled delightedly at one of the good looking young men at her table and bit into the corn. She felt her front teeth break off and stick into the ear. She didn't dare move the ear of corn away from her face because she would lose the teeth, and certainly didn't want these super "hunk" speakers to see her without her bridge. She held the cob of corn to her mouth with one hand, grabbed her purse with the other, and called a much-muffled "Bye!" as she ran like Cinderella from the room. The men stood up and called after her in bewilderment, "Aren't you going to dance?"

Lilly raced to the shuttlebus and rode it back to the deluxe hotel, through the glamorous lobby, still pressing the corn cob to her face.

Safe in her room she extracted the severed teeth, and made a dozen futile phone calls to dentists. Finally she persuaded the bellman to bring her some crazy glue. By morning the glue was dry and Lilly sang bravely through clenched teeth for the National Speakers Association, hoping her teeth would not pop out like popcorn on the high notes.

What If We Really Followed Instructions?

Some of the most successful speakers have taken the idea of laughing at themselves and used it to become rich and famous. A good example is Rosita Perez. Rosita does a spoof of the famous "happy marriage through subservience" book popular a few years ago. You remember that in it wives were advised to do all sorts of outlandish things to keep the spark of romance alive.

Rosita asks her audiences to contemplate, "What would *really* happen if we wrapped ourselves in saran wrap to meet our husbands at the door, trying to insure that they will not ask, "What's for dinner?"

You can imagine the laughter when Rosita explains that when she actually tried it, the book did not give her complete instructions. The happy marriage author did not explain that she should wrap each leg individually. Rosita took an old idea, gave it a comic twist, and come up with someting new and exciting that has her audiences howling with laughter.

Rosita and the saran wrap reminds me of the time our children finally got me up on a horse. Being of a practical turn of mind, I took a basket with me thinking I could reach the top branches of our avocado tree and bring in some hard-to-reach fruit. A good use for the horse, I thought.

Unfortunately the horse did not stop under the tree, but kept going. I yelled "Whoa!" just as I had seen the cowboys do in those western pictures.

The horse evidently had not seen the same movies I had. He kept moseying along with me frantically reaching for avocadoes until a big branch swept me, basket, and fruit all to the ground. My children have recounted the story of "Dottie Rides Again" hundreds of times, amid wild shrieks of laughter.

Mixing Real Life With Research

As a professional speaker I buy and greedily read every humor book, magazine and newsletter I can find. Visitors to our office have difficulty getting through the door because of the books, tapes and software. (Don't open the closet, please!) We hastily clear off a seat for guests. Our home and office are awash with stacks of books and tapes. How wonderful! An avalanche of ideas! I have always heard the voices in the books, ever since my mother left me at the Alhambra Public Library as a little girl because she could not afford a baby sitter. I feel at home, comfortable and contented if I have at least one stack of books in every room.

I use materials from quotation books, and a million other sources for my programs. My technique is to take a true story from my business life, add the new material to it, and weave it all into something new and wonderful for my audience. Here is a three-piece humor bit that originated in this manner:

1. I love business, hate cooking! When my children were small and I was running our advertising business, I told them "Get up, or I will cook breakfast!" (True story.)

2. As they grew older, I asked them what they would like me to make for dinner. Their firm answer—"Reservations!" (Material from joke source.)

3. In their teens I taught them my "red flag" system of scanning ads in newspapers and magazines to sell advertising. They learned to study the ads, make phone calls, pack my briefcase with the right samples and contracts, and appear in front of me with "Mom, we've got a hot one! Let's go eat and close the deal!" I taught my children how to look for and act on opportunities, to make a living, and to support their customers with their own purchases. (Passionate message).

The punch line of this piece of material is: "But I never did teach them to cook! (True story.) The fact is that all of the four children I have raised are delightful, funny cooks, who know how to laugh at life's problems. We come from a Celtic background, but our daughter Lilly's favorite creative concoctions are "Tuna, sauerkraut, bacon-bit burritos" and "Oyster cream cheese quesadillas."

You can see the California influence. The mere mention of the names of these outlandish dishes has made strong, hungry men blanche, then laugh hysterically. Lilly says the mere thought of her cooking actually helps their digestion, and frankly, they will need it. She says the men with character and courage stick around.

Read To the Children

Ever since our children were little we have read to them, and have tried to show them how to handle adversity. Often the first step to bouncing back from a blow is to see the funny side of the situation. We can compare our problem with that of a famous person from history, or a character in a play or book which helps to get a better perspective on it.

Since I read at least seven new books a week, our family conversation is often of books and ideas. My grown children greet me with, "What are you reading, Mom?" Often after they leave I search for the book we were discussing, and find it gone. Sure enough, they "borrowed" it. I am delighted. I wonder how mothers who do not read expect their children to love books? A book is very inexpensive. The love of books is invaluable.

As famous inspirational speaker Charles Tremendous Jones says: "What our character, spirit, and business will become five years from now depends on the books we read, the tapes we listen to, videos we watch, and the company we keep." The great biologist Lewis Thomas explains that thoughts enter our mind and travel on both an electric and chemical path. The thoughts have "prongs" on them he says. When they meet a similar thought they "dock" thus forming an aggregate. When the aggregate becomes large enough, we are forced to act. If we study pornography, or murder, we are building those aggregates in our minds. If we study humor, inspiration, and creative ideas, then those aggregates flourish and grow and leap forward to our aid when trouble arises, and we act in a positive way.

The Cherry Coke

If you could come into our office to visit with me today, you would see all across one side of the room a beautiful Spanish tile and mahogany soda fountain with nine leather-covered stools. Unusual? Yes. But if those stools could speak, they would tell you a story full of smiles.

It was a recession period, after World War II, jobs were scarce. Cowboy Bob, my husband, had purchased a small dry cleaning business. We had two darling babies, a tract home, car, and the usual time payments. Then the bottom fell out. There was no money for the house payments or anything else. Recession. People were being laid off. There were no jobs. Creditors kept calling on the phone and knocking on our door.

I felt that I had no special talent. I had no training, no college education. But I remembered someone in my past who thought I had a special talent, my Alhambra High School English teacher. She inspired me to take journalism and named me advertising manager and feature editor of the "Moor," our school paper. I remembered her in this financial emergency and thought, "Now if I could buy space from the small weekly newspaper in the town and resell it for a bit more, maybe I could make that house payment." But I had no car and no babysitter. I pushed my two children before me in a rickety stroller with a big pillow in the back and a wheel that kept coming off. I hit it back on with my shoe and kept going. I persuaded the newspaper publisher to let me have the first week's space at wholesale and on credit. I called on the merchants to sell my shopper's column ads.

The Idea Worked

I made enough money for the house payment and to buy an old used car Cowboy Bob found for me. Then I hired a high school girl to work from 3 to 5 each afternoon, babysitting. When the clock struck three

I grabbed my newspaper samples and flew out the door to drive to my telephone-made advertising sales appointments.

On one dark, rainy afternoon every prospect I had worked on turned me down. They told me that since the president of the Chamber of Commerce was not advertising in my shopper's column, there must be something wrong with it. The president owned the Baldwin Park Rexall Drug store, one of the most popular spots in town. Pharmacist Ruben Ahlman was my deadbolt. I could see that if he advertised with me, half of the other merchants in town would follow his lead. But each time I came in to the drug store he just shook his head from side to side. He even refused to speak to me on the phone.

But I was desperate. I decided on that dark afternoon to try again. Mr. Ahlman was at the prescription counter in the back of the store as I came in. I smiled my best smile, held up my newspaper with my shopper's column carefully marked in green crayola. He emphatically shook his head in that negative gesture again. "No." He was my key, but I couldn't get a grip on his mind to turn him.

Abandon All Hope?

Suddenly all my vigor left me. I made it as far as the beautiful old soda fountain at the front of the drug store and sat down on one of the stools, with the feeling that I didn't have the strength to drive home.

Mr Ahlman's ad would have meant the other merchants would buy, and this month's house payment would be covered. I pulled out my last dime and ordered a cherry coke, then put my head down on my hand and tried to swallow the tears welling in my eyes.

I hadn't noticed when I sat down, but at the next soda fountain stool sat a kind faced lady. She looked at me and put her hand on my arm. "What is the matter, dear?" she asked. I told her how much the people of the town revered the opinion of Mr. Ahlman, but he would not even look at my work. So now, I would lose the house. I didn't know where to turn. She took my newspaper with my column from my hand and said, "Let me read this."

I sipped my cherry coke sadly. Then suddenly the lady spun around and stood up. She stepped down from the soda fountain terrace, put her hands on her hips and yelled, "RUBIN AHLMAN, COME OUT HERE!"

She was Mrs. Ahlman, his wife! I learned that he was such a sweet, generous man, he bought everything that came along. So he had promised faithfully to shake his head "no." to everyone. Mr. and Mrs. Ahlman bought my ad, my tears were gone, we all laughed and smiled. The other merchants followed their lead. I made the house payment, and we often laughed about the turnaround of my life on that blessed revolving soda fountain stool.

Years later when the Ahlmans decided to take the soda fountain out of their store, my husband bought it, and he and our son installed it here in my office, where we offer cherry cokes and happy stories to the Speakers Bureau Clients and Speakers who come to visit us from all over the world.

Ben Winks At Me

As I began my advertising and speaking business, I read every business book I could find at the small Baldwin Park public library. I had only a high school education. But I decided "no college" did not have to mean "no learning." It was Frank Bettger, in his book, *How I Raised Myself From Failure to Success Through Selling*, who introduced me to his great friend of the mind, Ben Franklin. I remember there was a foil imprint of Ben Franklin's head on the front of the book. What a lucky day that was for me.

I decided that if Ben Franklin had so influenced Frank Bettger's success in business, I wanted to meet Ben too. I returned Bettger's book and picked up the "Autobiography of Benjamin Franklin." What a doorway to a treasure vault of great ideas! Today I have a whole set of shelves with books by and about Ben Franklin. My walls are lined with his pictures. Busts of Ben Franklin adorn the fireplace in my office. Whenever I have a business problem, I look up into his wise and twinkling eyes and think of how he would laugh at trouble, tell me a humorous story and a way to handle the situation. He closed almost every letter with, "And that will do the business."

I love his letter of encouragement to George Washington at Valley Forge. Ben was in France, raising money, troops and supplies for the newborn United States revolutionary army. Ben said, "George, keep your chin up. Smile at your men. If you could only see yourself as we see you from here. The miles between us are like years. We see you as the world of the future will see you. The great leader of a mighty new nation that will stand for individual freedom. Stand firm, George, stand firm."

Advice with a Chuckle

My darling Ben Franklin told me: "Dottie, never give up, just think of another way. And remember, when you want to persuade people, always talk of benefits to them, not yourself. Make them smile."

Ben was sent to England by the Colonies to get the hated Stamp Tax repealed after the famous tea-dumping in Boston Harbor. When Ben called on the English Lord in charge of the Colonies, he was kept standing outside the door. His business card was returned by the Butler: **"We are never at home to the Colonies,"** he was told.

Ben didn't stop. He took a big pad, wrote, "Resolved, The Stamp Tax on The Colonies Shall Be Reversed" across the top. He called first on good friends of the Colonies, carefully explaining the benefits to England by reversing the tax. Ben asked them to sign. Next he went to those who were sometimes friends. Many signed. Last, he spoke to those who were not considered friends. When they heard the benefits to England, and saw how many had already signed for repeal, they signed. He had enough signatures to place the issue before Parliament.

The day Parliament repealed the Stamp Tax, Ben was there. He said he was properly solemn and businesslike. But afterwards, since he wore the same suit he had worn when he was turned away on that first day, Ben **"noticed his suit was SMILING!"**

Trouble in Pomona

When I called on the Chamber of Commerce in Pomona to open a new territory for my young advertising business, they told me I must apply first to their "Secret Investigation Committee." I prepared recommendations, and filled out forms. A week later I received a letter from Mr. Bowen, owner of the big department store, as head of the "Secret Investigation Committee." He said, "We have turned you down."

I called and asked Mr. Bowen if I might come in and see him, thinking I must have failed to comply with some of their rules. I had no criminal record, was a United States citizen, and had a good sound business. I sat at his desk in a gold oak chair. "Please tell me the reasons, so that I may comply," I said earnestly.

"We give no reasons." he replied.

Outside in my car, I heard Ben Franklin whisper

in my ear, “Dottie, don’t give up. Think of another way.” I turned my car around the corner and immediately drove to the Pomona City Hall, walked in and asked to see the City Manager, Mr. Sharp. He listened attentively as I told him my story. Then he was angry: “Pomona encourages free enterprise. I want you to tell your story to the City Council.”

He explained that the city gave the Chamber of Commerce much money to promote new business. I did speak to the council and explained the benefits to the city’s commerce from my work. I told them about my business, and gave them my references. They promised to help me in every way they could, and approved my city license on the spot. My advertising business in Pomona flourished and was successful.

Watch for Changing Times

The Pomona Progress Bulletin newspaper ran a story about Mr. Bowen. He had retired as head of the department store, his son had now taken command. I reached for the phone and called for an appointment with his son. He invited me into his office where I sat in that same chair, wearing the same suit I had worn when his father had turned me away. I smiled and presented a very large advertising contract. I spoke only of positive benefits to the department store. Young Mr. Bowen smiled and signed my contract. He had a large check prepared, and handed it to me.

Outside in my car again, I saw the strangest thing: My suit was grinning!

Remember Funny Stories From Childhood

It is important to tell your children stories that have a purpose and a lesson, and especially a laugh. I use these stories for my audiences who love them too. If we use shallow and uninteresting stories, we lose the opportunity of delivering an inspiring message on the wings of humor.

This story is a favorite: When I was eight, my weekly goal was to get to the Saturday Matinee. There were cartoons, two big westerns, and hang-on-the-cliff serials, and often in those depression days, the theater gave you an ice milk bar on a stick as a bonus for the dime admission. Figuring out how to obtain those ten pennies to pay for the Saturday Matinee was a challenge.

It was sticky hot, the sultry dog days of August, before air conditioning. We didn't even have an electric fan. We kids cooled off with the garden hose, and ice chips struck from the big hunk of ice on the open back of the iceman's truck as he delivered to houses on our street. Then a big sign went up on a store that had been empty a long time. "LEO'S" it read. "Four scoops for 5 cents." We kids were agog. We couldn't believe it.

"Five, Five, Five Alive! Just FIVE cents!"

The news on the sign spread like wildfire. Four

BIG scoops! Twenty-five different flavors of ice cream! You only got two scoops for a nickel anywhere else. This cone soared! It towered! Magnificent! We all wanted one. We pressed our noses to the big glass store window and went over and over the endless list of flavors posted on the wall. What arguments we had over which combination was both most delicious and beautiful. I still remember all my favorite flavors; grape-pineapple, double chocolate, cherry-licorice, and caramel fudge.

Now I had two goals. Ten cents for the matinee, five cents for a towering cone. Then I smiled as an idea grabbed me.

A Plan

It took a full day to earn the first five pennies. I ran errands, sold bouquets of flowers from my backyard, tended babies. One penny was the going rate for go-fer jobs in those days. I never stopped askng, "Can I do something to help you? until I had all five cents. Then, clutching them in my hand, I walked proudly to Leo's, strutted past the other kids, through the door, and stood alone in front of his big flavor selection sign.

I went carefully and endlessly over his list of possibilities. It took a long, long time to choose. Each flavor had to be put on the cone in the right order so your taste buds could go from the chocolate fudge to the orange delight in the most perfect syncronization of delightful deliciousness. It took concentrated strategy.

Leo Anderson did not hurry me. He let me stand there in his cool store as long as I wanted, planning my color and flavor combinations. I remember his smile as he handed me my four scooper. “What a beauty!” he laughed, complimenting me on my rainbow selection. Oh, the thrill of it! I walked slowly and carefully back outside to the other kids.

The Four Scoop Deal

This is what I had figured out: “With a four scooper I was in a power position. I could negotiate all sorts of deals for a lick!”

I made the kids get in line, and traded licks for a penny, a comic book, jacks. No credit. Everyone watched closely while the buyers lick was taken. Straight up, no going around, no lingering. Ecstasy! But I discovered I had to have my lick deals lined up. Once melting began, time was crucial. I finally sold the cone filled with melted grape pineapple for the last penny. My four scooper was a step upward in my economic world. I turned those 5 pennies into 25, plus trade deals to boot. Then I tied the pennies into a hankie, keeping out 5 of them, and went in for another cone.

I learned good business from Leo. Give lots more, pressed down and overflowing. Make it unique. Smile. Be nice to your customers. Compliment their choice. Understand why they want it. Figure out how to do it for less. Add a new flavor often. Enjoy helping clients make their selections. Give them a four scoop deal!

And I had figured out that if people do not have the money to buy a whole thing, just cut it up into smaller portions and sell it so they can afford it, and earn a profit. Everybody wins, everybody smiles.

I have learned that the most important part of business is to put smiles on the faces of our customers, our audiences, our empoyees, and our families. This is not always done with material things. I love the words of Vince Lombardi, the great coach who said that in the heart of every player there is a dream and a hurt. He explained that when he focuses on either one, it grows. If he only sees the hurt, the player sickens and cannot play. If the coach concentrates on the dream, the player gets up and wins. Everyone smiles. I have read the life stories of many champions. They all worked to turn disaster into triumphs and smiles.

I hope you will like this poem I wrote about the great Babe Ruth, and how he smiled when he failed. Dr. Norman Vincent Peale wrote to me after he read it in our Speakers Magazine, *Sharing Ideas*, "Dear Dottie, Your poem is a masterpiece. You are a real poet...Babe Ruth had an outstanding philosophy—Just keep on swinging at it!"

Remember, concentrate on your dream. Everything else is dust. Shake it off, smile, concentrate and give it another whack.

UP AT BAT...

By Dottie Walters, C.S.P.

He crouched. The mighty Babe at bat!
His grip was strong and sure.
He said, "I aim the ball's small seam."
It flew at 90 per!

Babe swung so hard, if he had hit,
The ball would leave the park.
Instead the champ spun full around,
He fell. He'd missed his mark.

But Babe got up, brushed off the dust.
The spit a mouthful out,
Looked up and grinned a wondrous smile,
Let out a roaring shout.

"As long as I can stand, I'll swing!
My heart, my mind, my all.
I stack the odds each time I aim.
Don't count the times I fall."

Thoughts on Health & Humor

"Good Health and good sense
are two of life's greatest blessings."
- Publicus Syrus

"We are distinguished from all other creatures
by the faculty of laughter"
- John Addison

"There is no wealth above the wealth of health."
- Ben Sira

Your Thoughts on Health & Humor